· · · · ·
*The Ethics of Indeterminacy
in the Novels of William Gaddis*

. . . . .

The Ethics of Indeterminacy in the Novels of William Gaddis

Gregory Comnes

UNIVERSITY PRESS OF FLORIDA

Gainesville • Tallahassee • Tampa • Boca Raton
Pensacola • Orlando • Miami • Jacksonville

Library of Congress Cataloging-in-Publication Data

Comnes, Gregory.
The ethics of indeterminacy in the novels of William Gaddis /
Gregory Comnes.
    p. cm.
Includes bibliographical references (p.) and index.
ISBN 0-8130-1251-1 (alk. paper)
1. Gaddis, William, 1922— —Criticism and interpretation.
2. Ethics in literature. I. Title.
PS3557.A28Z64   1994   93-30650
813'.54—dc20   CIP

Portions of chapter 3 originally appeared in "Fragments of Redemption: Reading Gaddis's *J R*," in *Twentieth Century Literature* 35, no. 2. Reprinted by permission.

Portions of chapter 4 originally appeared in "A Patchwork of Conceits: Perspective and Perception in *Carpenter's Gothic*," in *Critique* 30, no. 1 (Fall 1988): 13–26. Reprinted by permission of the Helen Dwight Reid Educational Foundation. Published by Heldref Publications, 1319 18th Street, N.W., Washington, D.C. 20036-1802. Copyright 1988.

The University Press of Florida is the scholarly publishing agency for the State University System of Florida, comprised of Florida A & M University, Florida Atlantic University, Florida International University, Florida State University, University of Central Florida, University of Florida, University of North Florida, University of South Florida, and University of West Florida.

University Press of Florida
15 Northwest 15th Street
Gainesville, FL 32611

· · ·

For Judith, Jill, and Jonathan
who taught me how to love

Contents

Preface		ix
To Live Deliberately		1
1.	Ethics, Epistemology, and the Narrative of Indeterminacy	17
2.	The Recognitions	47
3.	*J R*	85
4.	*Carpenter's Gothic*	123
5.	Conclusion	147
Notes		151
Bibliography		163
Index		177

. . . . .
Preface

· · · The basis for what counts as knowledge traditionally has been the deep-rooted conviction that the real is unified and complete: chance, contingency, and error are conventionally considered signs that a particular theory is flawed and that a new, more "complete" theory is necessary.

But what if chance, contingency, and error are not flaws but are inherent in the system? What kind of theories would be possible in such a world, and how would one live in it meaningfully? These questions frame the inquiries of contemporary science and epistemology and are also questions that the novels of William Gaddis pose to the reader. Near the end of *Carpenter's Gothic* a character describes how fundamentalists perceive as threats "books that erode absolute values by asking questions to which there are no firm answers," a description that accurately describes Gaddis's narrative project. But although he makes every effort to erode absolute values, Gaddis also provides readers with a chance to consider what it means to have values without absolutes, eroding as well the suspicion that people cannot live meaningfully in a world that actively resists yielding firm answers.

* * *

Throughout this book's prolonged and complicated gestation I have received the help and advice of many people. Joseph Bentley and William Spengemann taught me the importance of thinking critically, though not their grace in using it. Steve Moore has been a fair-minded critic and friend, suggesting important revisions to my manuscript and helping to make sure this project reached completion. Special thanks go to Judith Chambers, whose combination of large-minded wisdom and generosity of spirit helped me learn what it means to live without absolutes.

* * *

Unless indicated otherwise, all ellipses in quotations from Gaddis's work are in the original texts.

· · · · ·

To Live Deliberately

I went to the woods because I wished to live deliberately, to front only
the essential facts of life, and see if I could not learn what it had to
teach, and not, when I came to die, discover that I had not lived.
—Thoreau, *Walden*

· · · To claim that ethics can serve as a meaningful subject
of contemporary narrative would be, it seems, to proceed isolated
from contemporary philosophy and ignorant of postmodern criticism. Conventional philosophical wisdom on the subject holds
that if ethics can be said to exist at all in this context it does so
as a derided object of nostalgia, a relic of logocentrism whose
quest will be subverted by the restrictions of language itself. This
is an age, as Robert N. Bellah reminds us in *Habits of the Heart*,
of disorder in moral discourse, when we speak "not one but several
moral languages"; a time Alasdair MacIntyre describes as one
when discussions of "right" and "wrong" are rendered trivial because of the "conceptual incommensurability" among the variety
of postmodern ethics.[1] In contemporary critical discourse, suspicion supersedes the sovereignty of normative evaluation, a time
of antitaxonomy when the normative distinctions we "naturally"
employ are seen as wobbly and arbitrary, not grounded in any
essence outside of language. The most ethical claim one can
make in this context is acknowledging the essential plurality of

the postmodern scene. It is no longer credible to argue that there exists a set of rules that legitimates prescriptive utterances taking precedence over other provinces of life, a belief succinctly stated by Jean-François Lyotard when he defines postmodernism as "an incredulity toward metanarrative."[2]

But if postmodernism reminds us of the obsolescence of the privileged text, the fraudulence of upholding the sovereignty of a consistent ethical discourse, it also supports the belief that utterances about reality are provisional, that laws plus chance equal postmodern reality, a statement whose truth is certified by the "chance" presence of the quite postmodern and quite ethical narratives of William Gaddis. When Jack Gibbs in Gaddis's *J R* is asked if his *Agapē Agape* manuscript is a novel, he responds, "—Not a, no no it's more of a book about order and disorder," a statement that just as accurately describes Gaddis's narrative project.[3] As postmodern texts, Gaddis's novels are ideologically sound in their presentation of a disordered world "agape": they reject what Leo Bersani in *The Culture of Redemption* identifies as the enervating and concealed morality of high modernism, the belief that innovation in aesthetic form in and of itself could transform social life, could provide a metanarrative solution.[4] Instead Gaddis's novels acknowledge what otherwise diverse manifestos agree is an important distinguishing characteristic of postmodernism—its vision of plurality and contingency.[5] Neither suppressing nor privileging the historical circumstances in which we live, Gaddis's narratives both acknowledge and exploit their own rhetorical status as fictions in affirming the essential indeterminacy of the postmodern scene. At the same time, these novels do not simply express an incredulity toward metanarrative, forgo morality altogether, and condemn readers to a deconstructive vision of senseless impasse that Albert Camus called "the absurd": "the appetite for the absolute and for unity and the impossibility of reducing this world to a rational and reasonable principle."

Instead, I hope to show that Gaddis helps us to construe sense and the possibility of order in a different way. Through his post-modern and radical version of ethics, what I will label the "ethics of indeterminacy," Gaddis shows how ethical choice, rather than conformity and passivity, is possible, even when the absolute has been replaced with the probable as the basis for judgment.

Our postmodern world, Gaddis reminds us in all three of his novels, is informed by "the unswerving punctuality of chance" (*Recognitions* 9, *J R* 486, *Carpenter's Gothic* 9), a statement acknowledging the fundamental gap between theory and experience.[6] In the course of a rare interview in *Paris Review*, Gaddis clarified the ethical implications of this statement, explaining that at the heart of his fiction "is precisely this courage to live without Absolutes, which is really, nothing more than growing up, the courage to accept a relative universe and even one verging upon chance."[7] This does not mean, however, that our "chance" world is absurd, at least in the conventional sense that Camus meant it. Rather, Gaddis returns us to the Latin root *surdus*, meaning deaf, making the point clear through J R's comments in the last lines of the novel: "Hey? You listening . . . ?" (*J R* 726). People can act meaningfully, but only if they are willing to grow up, which in part means setting aside the absolutes that make one deaf to the world, which remains unharmonious and cannot be understood through conventional systematizing.

To accomplish this one must have the courage, as Gaddis again reminds us in all three of his novels, "to live deliberately" (R 900, J R 477, C's G 139), the guiding principle of *Walden*.[8] Like Thoreau, another exponent of listening, Gaddis asks readers "to consider the way in which we spend our lives," to accept the importance of the virtue of alterity, that self-knowledge is linked with facts outside oneself. For Thoreau, ethical action meant setting aside habits and customs and embarking on a voyage to discover that "the Universe is wider than our views of it" (W

2:352). If one simplifies, one will hear the truth that "the laws of nature are not indifferent, but forever on the side of the most sensitive" (W 2:242).

But although he supports the importance of alterity, Gaddis rejects Thoreau's belief that if one set aside the self and lived deliberately one could discover the natural laws that would support the development of the "sensitive" man's spirit. Our universe is "relative," and if we do as Thoreau suggests and "listen to every zephyr for some reproof, for it is surely there" (W 2:242), the issue is cacophonous. In a world informed by "the unswerving punctuality of chance," Gaddis calls into question what Thoreau simply assumed, the very possibility of living "deliberately" as an act of discovery. Today Walden has been plumbed, packaged, and sold, transfigured by a pervasive commodity fetishism that has penetrated the heretofore impregnable human realms of imagination and psyche championed by Thoreau. Gaddis makes this point clear by reducing the status of Thoreau's dictum in the progression of his novels from the protagonist's clear intention in *The Recognitions* to a flip aside about monogrammed doormats in *J R*, culminating in *Carpenter's Gothic* as a literal fiction uttered by a fictional character inside a novel written by a character whose own ethical status is problematic. In so doing, Gaddis reminds readers that the status of "to live deliberately" is not given but provisional, an act not of discovery but of invention, synonymous with and contingent on the willingness of the person to risk enacting it in a world informed by chance and militant ignorance in equal measure.

To grow up, then, means to accept not only the virtue of alterity but also those virtues of risk and responsible suffering that together form the critical attitude that the postmodern world requires us to assume to live without absolutes. This is the ethics of indeterminacy I will trace in Gaddis's novels, an ethic where "to live deliberately" means seeking to recover some provisional sense of _agapē_ in a world that remains intractably "agape."

(A cautionary note on the term _agapē_ and its variants: Throughout this book I will deliberately avoid any discussion of _agapē_ love in the situation of the Christian believer. Reading Gaddis makes it clear that his concern is not with any conventional Christian doctrine—except as the object of satire—but rather with the general structure of a consciousness informed by the virtues of alterity, risk, and responsible suffering.)

To establish how the ethics of indeterminacy serves as the central concern of Gaddis's work, I will assume a somewhat different perspective than do other readers of Gaddis. In the face of the exasperating allusiveness of his first two novels, _The Recognitions_ and _J R_, critics have tended to read these works as separate sourcebooks, collections of arcane references that, when glossed sufficiently, will provide an understanding of what the books mean.[9] Although helpful in dispelling many of the earlier and at times errant readings of Gaddis's work, such scholarship for the most part has not yet provided answers to the more complex and more important questions of why these novels take the form they do and what thematic progression they might follow.[10] More recent critics have started to read Gaddis from the poststructuralist perspective that meaning lies in the way the author uses language. Most notable in this regard is John Johnston's _Carnival of Repetition_. This study, which explores the intertextual maze of _The Recognitions_ through Bakhtin's theory of the dialogic novel and Deleuze's logic of the simulacrum and phantasm, makes clear how for Gaddis "intertextuality was a compositional feature from the outset."[11] Even so, Johnston limits his study to how Gaddis presents a world without absolutes, choosing not to place these linguistic experiments in the ethical context of how one can _live_ in such a world, a context that I argue remains central to Gaddis's narrative project.[12] Thus, although I agree that Gaddis acknowledges the poststructuralist claim that language is conceptually limited in its ability to mean, this limitation does not preclude the possibility of recovering meaning linguistically. Instead, I argue that Gaddis uses language in a way analogous to that of contemporary epistemology, a way that includes nonconceptual linguistic modes of participation and experience and opens the door to the possibility of a postmodern agapistic ethics.

The basis of this study, then, is that understanding Gaddis's narrative project means understanding he has written what I term epistemological novels, narratives whose form is keyed to the epistemological concerns of a particular age and generates a commensurate ethical vision. Although all fiction is preconditioned to some degree by these concerns, Gaddis's novels do not simply allude to these principles. Instead, they employ the epistemological concepts as principles of composition, incorporating into fictive modes of discourse the conditions imposed on the nature of meaning by the reigning postmodern epistemology of indeterminacy. In creating a body of narrative methods whose characteristics reflect this principle, the form of the novels instructs the reader how the recovery of meaning is possible within a contingent textual landscape. At the same time, I will also argue that Gaddis's novels are ethically compelling because they provide some warrant for believing that this epistemological view also applies to human experience, that the form of these novels also shows us how to read our postmodern world and recover ethical meaning within it.

In considering these claims, one might ask why I have made no effort to locate Gaddis's work in a larger context of postmodern American writing, if I am hopelessly naive in apparently claiming a mimetic form for any postmodern novel, or whether such critical scaffolding as the "epistemological novel" is truly necessary to help grasp what Gaddis is saying. Writers from Acker to Pynchon certainly also consider the issues of ethics and love in our time, and many would sympathize with the trenchant claim made by Jerome Klinkowitz that postmodern theory must reject mimesis as a significant mode of presentation: "If the world is absurd, if what passes for reality is distressingly unreal, why spend time representing it?"[13] And can it really be said that the epistemological demands Gaddis's books place on their readers require labeling any more specialized than the truism applicable to virtually all postmodern literature—difficult books always teach their readers the virtue of hard work?

As to the first point, love as a topic does make an occasional appearance in postmodern literature, most notably in the work of Thomas Pynchon. Judith Chambers, for example, insightfully argues that a central issue of Pynchon's oeuvre is his concept of "a postmetaphysical ethics, a basis for humane action, that is located not in a set of prescriptive rules but rather in the indeterminate, contingent, though not subjective principle of love."[14] She maintains that this ethic cannot be found in Pynchon's rare exhortations to "keep cool, but care" or to believe that amidst a ruined landscape "love occurs."[15] Instead, it is revealed through what she describes as the reader's encounter with a narrative in *Gravity's Rainbow*, which restores "the enigmatic, mysterious poetic faculty to thinking." By engendering both a skepticism toward reductive systems and an openness to experience, such an encounter provides readers with a narrative experience that is in itself "the morphological equivalent of love."[16] In contrast, Gaddis, who shares Pynchon's rejection of facile generalizations, clearly delineates the quality of love in his work by taking as the central issue of all his novels a specific moral incommensurability that is a product of a particular historical conjunction in American culture, explained succinctly by Jack Gibbs in *J R* as "can't escape this god-damned protestant ethic have to redeem it" (477).

This allusion to Max Weber's *The Protestant Ethic and the Spirit*

of Capitalism helps to explain the two poles—*agapē* and agape—
of Gaddis's postmodern version of America's incommensurate
ethic and the circumstances necessary for redeeming it. I argue
that on one hand Gaddis's novels present ethics in terms of
Luther's notion of calling: to live religiously in this world, to
look on the secular life as affording opportunities to express the
duty of love to one's neighbor. In this sense, virtue is seen as a
solution to problems with human egoism, and the content of
morality equates with alterity, an *agapē* love that places an absolute emphasis on others.

On the other hand, Gaddis's novels also admit the existence
of another calling, the ethical obligation of Weber's capitalist to
make money. In contrast to the virtues of love, this calling defines
the good as the bureaucratic efficiency of self-interest, a cost
versus benefit equation that, in understanding every facet of life
as a commodity, invariably stands agape—what Weber described
as depersonalized—at the humanitarian ideal of loving one's
neighbor as oneself.

In presenting the pluralistic callings of the Protestant ethic in
our postmodern culture, Gaddis also shows readers that redemption cannot mean simply reconciling this moral incommensurability by looking to the rules of traditional morality to justify separating oneself from the pernicious evil of an avaricious society. Such
thinking is naive and, when acted upon by characters, ultimately
destructive: in the face of the power of our cultural bureaucracy
to conceal and dissemble its arbitrary workings, Gaddis shows it
to be omnipresent and inescapable, part of a complementary ethic
that intractably resists further reduction. Instead, redemption
must include submitting to the authority of experience, a submission that acknowledges the endurance of the bureaucratic good
and recognizes that any offsetting moral principle of loving one's
neighbor must include its successful execution in the bureaucratic

world to have meaning; otherwise the ethic will remain "god-damned" insofar as love is absent from it.

Redemption, then, is contingent upon action, a redemption whose realization I argue emerges from a third calling—actions that the participating reader, prompted by the blueprint of the texts' language, chooses to perform. The message of redemption thus becomes in part the idea that redemption has not been adequately defined as long as analyzing a text—linguistic or worldly—has not moved from a rhetorical to an existential realm, a shift from character to reader as the locus of development. If the reader is willing to risk taking the responsibility to make this move, then he can, by transforming the various linguistic discontinuities into some provisional meaning, also learn how to recover some semblance of meaning in the world the language of the novels reflects. The texts become teacher, legitimating first how learning a certain set of epistemological procedures can yield literary meaning, then legitimating the extrapolation of these procedures to the human realm, specifically as a form of love that just might redeem this "god-damned" ethic.

In claiming that Gaddis's postmodern novels exhibit a naturalistic is/ought ethics—one that justifies moral principles in terms of epistemological concepts—I assert that Gaddis's novels are mimetic in their capacity to recognize and produce similarities—between both text and world and epistemology and ethics—but not mimetic in the reductive and pejorative sense Jerome Klinkowitz suggests. Instead, I argue that Gaddis's novels represent what Derrida describes as *mime*, a "new mimesis" that recasts the text rather than an outside referent as the object of study.[17] Drawing on the language theory of Walter Benjamin, whose relevance to Gaddis is analyzed at length in chapters 1 and 3, I understand Gaddis's mimetic form to be what Benjamin describes as "nonsensuous similarity."[18] As did Benjamin, Gaddis floods his works with fragments, a montage of quotations and allusions inserted not so that the reader can fabricate a recuperative strategy but instead so that readers can grasp what Benjamin describes as "the dialectic at a standstill" through a text designed "to collect and reproduce in quotation the contradiction of the present without resolution."[19]

The purpose of this technique is twofold. First, following Benjamin's strategy, Gaddis's texts call into question the assumed validity of the activity of textual reference, displacing the concept of referent from unquestioned method to problematized subject, what Benjamin described as the "outdated meditation between two different filing systems."[20] This mode of representation in turn recasts the idea of how one makes a text intelligible. Because Gaddis's texts substitute heterogeneous example for argument and explanation to such a degree, the reader is forced to approach the object of study in a different way, one where the textual intelligibility becomes a product of the reader's willingness to participate in the text's principle of composition by transferring the writer's invention theory from the writer's fiction to the reader's critical understanding. By enacting or miming this principle, the reader "performs" the text, interweaving what Benjamin describes variously as "traces" and "fragments" of relationships. In Benjamin's theory such language itself becomes a medium of experiencing the world, "the most perfect archive of nonsensuous similarity," and reading becomes a form of action, of risk-taking to read that which is embedded in fragmentary form.[21] To be sure, the path to this experience is difficult, involving what Benjamin saw as an archaeology of exploration and destruction on the part of the reader, but the path is still negotiable. As a result, the reader of Gaddis confronts a work that actively and self-consciously promotes its ideology of essential indeterminacy. The reader becomes the primary ethical agent engaged in an aforementioned third calling: reading the novels as events, unfolding experientially an understanding of what sort of procedures are necessary "to live deliberately." In so doing the reader learns to enact an agapistic ethics of indeterminacy in a postmodern landscape and to recover through hermeneutic exploration and risk and dialogical transactions a redemption that necessarily remains open to further risk-taking.

Insofar as my analysis of ethics in Gaddis's postmodern narrative stresses form and specific (albeit provisional) solutions, my conclusion differs from the more general analyses reached by critics such as Alec McHoul and Alan Wilde concerning what McHoul describes as the condition of the "post-ethical" in contemporary narrative.[22] Both suggest that postmodern ethics—if they can be understood at all in narrative—can at most provide what Wilde explains as "suspensive irony": "the world in all its disorder is simply (or not so simply) accepted."[23] Gaddis, I argue, also accepts the radical vision of the essential indeterminacy of postmodernism. But instead of settling for acceptance, or McHoul's definition of the postmodern ethical act as the "refusal of ethics," Gaddis's work provides both definitions of value and specific methods of recovering these values in both the disordered landscape of Gaddis's fiction and the disordered world it represents, definitions and methods requiring specific labeling to clarify how Gaddis puts them to use.[24]

The specific subject, the experience of which is enfolded in Gaddis's nonsensuous language, is contemporary epistemology, what I label essential indeterminacy. This epistemology, which I will explain primarily in terms of its emergence in quantum physics, acknowledges both the formal undecidability of principles—that concepts have only regulative rather than constitutive status in generating knowledge—and the necessary role experience plays in the construction of meaning. In this context the hard work Gaddis's novels require takes on a special significance beyond the inevitable difficulty involved in reading avant-garde texts. The narrative enactment of this epistemology shows readers how hard work is a necessary precondition for having meaning in narrative by forcing readers to participate actively in the construction of narrative meaning, requiring them to bring information to the text to read what was never written. In a sense, Gaddis, an admirer of Eliot's *Four Quartets*, confronts readers with the nonlyrical quotidian middle ground necessarily absent from Eliot's crystalline verse.[25] The general themes of both authors are similar: consciousness not through illumination but through exploration, as the fruit of suffering whose price is paid in small coinage, day by day. But to make the move from Gaddis's version of "East Coker" to "Little Gidding," to make the journey "wherein there is no ecstasy" in order "to arrive at where we started / And know the place for the first time," requires that the readers themselves plunge into Gaddis's massive narrative version of "The Dry Salvages," a three-novel "trial by water" that, consisting of "only hints and guesses, / Hints followed by guesses," requires readers to assemble what is necessary to regain meaning under conditions, as Eliot describes, that do indeed "seem unpropitious." Understanding can result—reflecting essential indeterminacy in narrative does not mean assuming the imitative fallacy of unnarratable postmodern epistemology—but the status of understanding is provisional, dependent upon the reader's willingness to go beyond a vision of a finished text whose message is retrospectively perceived. This trope of indeterminacy shows that narrative meaning, like meaning understood by contemporary epistemology, is not inherent—antecedent of experience and absolute. Instead, meaning is provisional—synonymous with and contingent on the action of readers willing to take seriously Gaddis's reminder in *J R*: "Don't bring a God-damned thing to it can't take a God-damned thing from it" (605). Further, because these qualities are also the fundamental components of the agapistic ethic Gaddis champions in the content of his novels, I also show that these techniques function to remind readers how the willingness to forgo absolutes and still take action is necessary for the possibility of redemptive love in a moral realm of formal undecidability—our postmodern worldly text of "*agapē* agape."

My justification for labeling these novels "epistemological"— works using epistemological principles as organizing concepts that confer value through literary experience—finds its inspiration in the narrative theories of Hermann Broch. Trained as a philosopher, Broch nevertheless forsook the positivist philosophy of the early twentieth century for what he termed *Dichtung*, or "creative literary activity."[26] For Broch, *Dichtung* took the form of a novel, one "that delves back behind psychological motivation to basic epistemological attitudes and to the actual logic and plausibility of values."[27] Broch's epistemological novel became the force to voice what was described as meaningless in positivist terms—the cognition (*Erkenntis*) of human reality in terms of ethical behavior. "History is composed of values," wrote Broch, "yet these values cannot be introduced into reality as absolutes, but can only be thought of in reference to an ethically motivated value-positing subject."[28]

Despite his rejection of positivistic science, however, Broch's theory of knowledge required that the epistemological innovations of the time, especially the then-new theory of relativity, be incorporated into any novel designed to instruct man how to find an ethical dimension in the twentieth century. Broch used science not as a casual reference but instead to shape the principles of his narrative. The most famous example of this influence is found in *The Sleepwalkers*, a polyhistorical novel Broch structured around what he described as the "narrator as idea," specifically using the idea of relativity as a narrator to shape the multiperspectival, fragmented, and discontinuous nature of his narrative.[29] Because he incorporated this epistemological theory as a principle of narrative composition, Broch felt that the reader would perforce learn how this otherwise abstract theory operates in the world of man, how explanations of reality might also operate as guidelines for ethical conduct otherwise dominated by the reductionist ethics of positivism.

In showing how Gaddis employs this concept of using epistemology to confer value in his own novels (Gaddis specifically refers to *The Sleepwalkers* in *J R*), I also illustrate how Gaddis's fiction provides some warrant for believing that the particular epistemological view of postmodernism applies to the human experience of values. Insofar as they embody pertinent explanations of the essential indeterminacy of contemporary epistemology, Gaddis's epistemological novels extend and refine what Broch proclaims throughout *The Sleepwalkers* as the dilemma of man caught between the "no longer and the not yet," between the breakdown of an old system and a new one not yet crystallized. To survive in this *Grenzsituation*, a border situation when the sense of breakdown is far greater than in Broch's time, we must become participants in what both Frederic Jameson and Umberto Eco refer to as "guerilla warfare."[30] Each advocates attacking the forces of suppression and privilege while championing an open-minded and tolerant attitude toward essential indeterminacy, what John Caputo describes as "coping with the flux" of the postmodern era.[31] Gaddis's narrative enactment of contemporary epistemology allows such participation, for it teaches readers a method of recovering meaning—what I will identify as Gaddis's particular notion of *agapē* ethics—that is as applicable to the border situations of our essentially problematic social world as it is to an essentially problematic text.

Because the epistemological basis of the ethics of indeterminacy is such a slippery subject, one good way to clarify the nature of this basis, the ethics that derives from it, and the narratives that refer to it is to show how each contributes to the form of Gaddis's postmodern epistemological novels. This comparison forms the basis for chapter 1, where the foundations for and the specific nature of essential indeterminacy, its ethic, and its trope are established. Following the essay on the epistemological novel are three chapters, one each on *The Recognitions*, *J R*, and *Carpenter's Gothic*. By applying the formal concept of the epistemological novel to these works, the analysis of each novel aims to explain how the novels mean, why certain elements appear in the order and form they do. My concern is not to read exhaustively each of Gaddis's novels: Steven Moore has already engaged in the Herculean task of plowing through the thickets of Gaddis's prose with a remarkable combination of thoroughness, clarity, and insightfulness.[32] Rather, my goal is to delineate a set of narrative methods so that informed readers can then read the novels for themselves, deriving (as I believe Gaddis intends) how the idea of postmodern ethics in these novels is grasped through experiencing the texts rather than reading criticism about them. If my analysis of how these novels mean holds water, it should help to clarify how at least one postmodernist writer can provide an honest vision of an essentially indeterminate landscape, a postmodern world without absolutes, while providing the means for readers to courageously seek to discover meaning and value within it.

1 · · · · ·

Ethics, Epistemology, and the
Narrative of Indeterminacy

Let no man join what God has put asunder.
—*Wolfgang Pauli*

· · · In laying claim to the idea that Gaddis's novels enact epistemological concepts in narrative form to clarify ethics, stating some basic assumptions is in order. Because the intent here is not to debate axiology but rather to clarify how the ethics of indeterminacy informs Gaddis's narratives, the working definition of morality will be deliberately kept simple: a system that describes man as he is, a vision of man as he should appear, and a set of principles designed to move him from the first to the second realm. The point is not to see morality as Aristotelian, or Kantian, or Utilitarian, but to view it as a certain attribute whose possession is part of what is deemed to be human. In the case of Gaddis's narratives, this means having the courage to live deliberately, putting oneself in another's place in a world without absolutes: to practice what will be explained in this chapter as living in the state of *agapē* in a world that is agape. This is not to say, however, that this discussion of morality proceeds innocent of historical debate on the subject. My explanation of Gaddis's ethics rests on the arguable assumption in philosophy that fundamental values in any culture should be coherent with the metaphorical structure of the most fundamental concepts of understanding in that culture. Running counter to G. E. Moore's dictum in *Principia Ethica*, that moral terms cannot be defined in terms of nonmoral realities, I will argue that Gaddis's morality is naturalistic and pragmatic, that it assumes, as Richard Rorty describes, a significant connection between *is* and *ought*: "There is no epistemological difference between truth about what ought to be and truth about what is, nor any metaphysical difference between facts and values, nor any methodological difference between morality and science."[1]

Rorty's position certainly has history on its side, because science, the most forceful spokesperson for epistemology since Descartes, has traditionally provided the reasonable foundation for ethical action—the idea that the perceived natural order provides the foundation for everyday moral thinking. The power of scientific explanation, linked with the turn to secularism and the spirit of revolution, has insured modern humanity's scientific belief about reality impinges on action guidelines, whether it be an ethical order fixed by the static nature of the eighteenth century, the swell of progress (and the slough of despond) ushered in by the evolutionary nature of the nineteenth century, or the sense of fatalism defined by the entropic nature of the twentieth century, at least as seen by Henry Adams. The idea that any modern ethical theory cannot be understood apart from accounts of the epistemological conditions for its emergence is so prevalent that it appears to be, as Lovin and Reynolds describe it in *Cosmogony and Ethical Order*, a transcultural phenomenon, where "individuals relate their basic notions of the origins of the reality in which they live their lives to the patterns of actions that they consider to be dependable and worthy of choice."[2] In *The Return to Cosmology*, Stephen Toulmin furthers this idea when he comments that man's ambition "to find 'a cosmic sanction for ethics,' a 'natural foundation on which our human superstructure of right and wrong may safely rest,' is an enduring one."[3]

However much epistemological concerns play a necessary part in making ethics coherent with the fundamental concepts of a culture, the fact that Gaddis presents his agapistic ethics of indeterminacy in narrative form suggests that epistemology alone is not sufficient to the task. Gaddis, in the words of Iris Murdoch, clearly believes that the most coherent moral philosophy should be inhabited, dramatized to get man out from "under the net" of complacency generated when one thinks about the "facts" of ethical theory to remember that we also learn to be moral by hearing other people's stories and that nothing can cohere independent of the way people use and understand through language.[4] Some aspects of the good can't be formulated in explicit rules, a phenomenon Michael Polyani calls "tacit knowledge" that is gained through practice and cannot be articulated explicitly.[5] Instead, these aspects of ethical behavior need to be dramatized, played out in narratives that are mundane in the sense that they take man and society as their subject, establishing some basis for action amidst the perplexities of life rather than of theory. In this narrative context, ethics are best described as eclectic, not as a set of ideas that precedes and informs action but that arises from complications whose presentation is more suited to the realm of narrative. Philosophical treatises on ethics tend to assume that all men live in the same empirical, rationally comprehensible, impersonal world and that morality is the adoption of universal and openly defensible rules of conduct. John Rawls's *A Theory of Justice*, for example, has received high praise in philosophical circles for arguing how a fair system of justice can result when parties, having moved to a fiction of an "Original Position," choose principles from behind a "veil of ignorance" that keeps them from knowing how their choices might benefit them person-

ally.[6] Rawls brackets rational humanity to clarify how his contrac-
tualist theory of ethics is possible. Ethics that issues forth from
narrative, in contrast, problematizes the assumption of man's
inherent rationality in order to clarify man's tendency in practice
to ignore contracts. In substituting example for argument, narrative reminds readers that the moral world is populated with other
persons who, in their eccentricity and opacity, redefine the parame-
ters of the veil of ignorance. In *After Virtue*, one of the more lucid
commentaries on the condition of postmodern ethics, Alasdair
MacIntyre focuses on the epistemological significance of dramatic
narrative to the possibility of having a postmodern ethics.[7] At a
time when moral concepts exist without contexts, McIntyre argues that no theory should be presented neutrally but instead
should be presented in a frankly subjective way, as a plot whose
form involves an evaluative judgment that champions humanity's
freedom from oppressive constraints.

The value of presenting ethics in a narrative context appears
to be twofold. First, it enacts propositions in the contexts of
peoples' lives, reminding us how schemes that are preachy, censo-
rious, or theory-laden inevitably distort or reduce the world to
which they are applied. Part of the power of presenting ethics in
narrative, then, is to manifest an anticanonical stance, a hermeneutics of suspicion that exposes nostalgia as a residue of outmoded
views, a residue that promises to console but that really disables,
creating not so much illusion as delusion. The ethical point is that
these views are exposed not simply because they are wrong but because they hinder humanity's possibilities of well-being.

A second corrective function offered by the narrative presentation of ethics is to demolish any remnants of the western ideal
of people as rational decision makers who adjudicate according
to a set of ideals, reminding us that any theory is open to question
in the ongoing context of life and that we must be on guard
against even our most trusted analysis of how things are. Unlike

theory, narrative is well suited for presenting the deformations to which ethics are liable: the shift from rational duty to pathological habit, how morality can become a way to perfect man's slavery, and that strangest of all human phenomena, self-destructiveness.

From the above analysis, it seems clear that a most compelling answer to the question of what should we do lies in asking the right questions: discovering of what story we are a part and finding some way of accommodating both epistemological explanation and human justification by tying together the narrative derived from the order of things with a narrative of how people might live in this world, forever suspicious of theorizing.

William Gaddis, in addressing this issue of knowledge and its function in the format of postmodern ethical narrative, keeps us asking the right questions by writing what I call epistemological novels, works that accurately recast the epistemology of postmodernism in narrative guise. But simply to say that narrative explains an epistemological system by putting it in a humanly usable form does not in itself throw much light on the subject of what makes Gaddis's work cosmological: almost all narratives, in all ages, have tried to draw some comprehensible conclusion about the external world. Gaddis's narratives do not simply refer to a particular explanation of reality, however; they also refer to that explanation in different ways—ways dictated by and appropriate to the conditions imposed on language by that particular world view. Before turning to the details of how this works, however, it is first necessary to explain in more detail the reigning epistemological sensibility of the postmodern era.

*   *   *

In using the principles of quantum physics to talk about postmodern epistemology, I do not mean to argue the philosophic truth claims of these concepts as epistemic justification theories but rather to show how the worldview projected by theories of quantum physics has plausibly exerted some influence on what counts as knowledge.[8] Nevertheless, it remains true that since the advent of modern times, science has been regarded, rightly or wrongly, as an important part of the epistemic justification of reality, a reality explained most often through the language of physics. What follows, then, argues the plausibility of both how the projected worldview of quantum physics has influenced epistemology and how these epistemological concerns serve as the focus of Gaddis's ethical narratives. By making this argument I also seek to avoid the error, all too common in books on the subject, of simply stipulating a connection between quantum physics and postmodern narratives, then making sweeping claims based on this stipulation.[9] Finally, to minimize overgeneralizing a complex subject, the following explanation is limited to but one key issue of postmodern physics—its concept of anomaly as contrasted with Newtonian physics and the implications that emerge for a postmodern ethics in a world of essential indeterminacy.

Newtonian mechanics rest on the assumption of a nature out there that can be, at least in principle, completely explained by an objective observer. Whenever an anomaly occurs in the mechanism, the premise that all events have a cause that can be determined by listing all the antecedent conditions generates a theory that in its identification, clarification, and explanation of the anomaly reconstructs the broken symmetry. Like Augustine's concept of evil, anomalous events in Newtonian terms are in effect privations of an explanation of the universe that is good: complete, consistent, and objective. People can, of course, make errors in theorizing, but the ideal of describing nature completely and objectively remains intact.[10] In the Newtonian dispensation, the universe is just that—a realm of logic and law whose fundamental unity is revealed through the magic of what is called algorithmic compressibility, a pattern of logic that allows observed data to be represented in a truncated form while possessing the same information content. As John Barrow describes it in *A Theory of Everything*, "normal" Newtonian science, insofar as it seeks closure, is nothing but the seeking out of algorithmic compression: "Science is predicated upon the belief that the Universe is algorithmically compressible and the modern search for a Theory of Everything is the ultimate expression of that belief, a belief that there is an abbreviated representation of the logic behind the Universe's properties that can be written down in finite form by human beings."[11]

Barrow concludes that however compelling the idea may be, there is no theory of everything that can satisfy all received observations in the contemporary explanatory mode.[12] His conclusion underscores contemporary science's general belief that the principle of objective and complete knowledge has been superseded, in the sense that what Newtonian theory called anomaly is no longer considered to be a privation. Instead, the notion of anomaly is now considered inherent in scientific explanations of reality. Science now admits that theory itself is at best partial, an epistemological restriction imposed not by present limits of measurement but by both the nature of the world and the nature of theory. To the notion of algorithmic compression, science must now add what complexity theory identifies as algorithmic transcomputability, the realization that there are situations in which the computational costs exceed all bounds that govern the physical implementation of algorithms, costs determined by the fundamental limits of signal flow dictated by the uncertainty principle of quantum mechanics.[13] The implications of this concept are profound. If one can assume that the universe is bound by physical laws and that the laws of mathematics and logic are inexpressible without implementing algorithms, then anomaly is inherent in explanations of reality at the highest levels. To understand the revolution generated by the acceptance of anomalies that cannot be resolved into more fundamental order, it is instructive to consider the two major events in the history of science that allow this acceptance: the redefinition of the logic of theory and the recognition of the significant role played by such subjective factors as bias and even belief in the practical application of theory.

The idea that theory itself is forever limited by internal logical constraints was first put forth by the German mathematician Kurt Gödel. Gödel's theorem appears as Proposition VI in his 1937 paper, "On formally undecidable propositions in *Principia Mathematica* and related systems." The theorem reads as follows: "To every *W*-consistent recursive class of *K* of formulae there correspond recursive *class-signs* r, such that neither v Gen r nor Neg (u Gen r) belongs to Fly (k) (Where v is the free variable of r)."[14]

Despite the formidable title and the terminology of symbolic logic, the concept itself is straightforward enough, in effect stating that all consistent axiomatic formulations of number theory include undecidable propositions. The significance of this concept to the creation of theories of mathematical logic is as follows. Prior to Gödel, the assumption was that a system of mathematical logic could be both consistent (contradiction-free) and complete (i.e., every true assertion of the theory could be derived from the framework of the theory). Gödel's incompleteness theorem showed the impossibility of formulating such a theory that was at once consistent and complete. In the post-Gödelian world, a theory would be either consistent by virtue of leaving out information or else it would be complete at the expense of allowing internal inconsistencies. In either case, the theory would be limited by anomalous conditions not subject to further refinement.

The profound philosophical implications of Gödel's theorem are readily apparent: if the ideal logical system of numbers as Gödel's theorem describes it is itself either inherently incomplete or inconsistent, can any theory of reality describe an unchanging truth? One possible answer is that in actual practice, Gödel's theorem does not impose consequential limits on most areas of experimental scientific inquiry. As long as the axiomatic system is not as large as the whole of arithmetic, it will not be subject to Gödel's incompleteness. Such is the case, for example, in Presburger arithmetic, which in limiting itself to operations on positive whole numbers and zero allows all of its properties to be decidable.[15] Further, Gödel's theorem does not theoretically preclude complete and consistent inquiries into the realm of nature, because the referents of scientific sentences, unlike those of arithmetic, lie outside of language and many questions concerning anomalies are ultimately decided by observation rather than by logic.

This belief in objects that run their course in space and time according to causal laws regardless of whether or not one observes them has, however, been repudiated by another aspect of the new explanatory cosmological mode, quantum mechanics.[16] That there is a limit to objectivity and completeness even within physics, traditionally the most stringent of the sciences, is best expressed by two famous concepts.

The first of these, the uncertainty principle formulated by Werner Heisenberg in 1927, states that the position and momentum of subatomic particles are complementary qualities that can only be approximated, not known. As one variable is measured with greater precision, the value of the other becomes more indeterminate. More important, such imprecision is not a function of the limitation of present instruments but rather an inherent property of nature itself, one marked by the length of Planck's constant.[17] Although this distance (6.77×10^{-27} meters) is infinitesimal, the fact that this degree of uncertainty cannot be circumvented through the use of more sophisticated probes marks the limits of observation, not logically, as Gödel's theorem did, but ontologically.

The second pertinent disruption of the objective determinism of Newtonian common-sense physics appears in the form of Niels Bohr's concept of complementarity. In his famous depiction of the nature of light as both particle and wave, Bohr conclusively demonstrated that the so-called objective world of fact is conditioned by the experiments humans choose to perform.[18] The particle-like behavior of light observed in one kind of experiment is not a property of light; it is a property of one's interaction with light. Similarly, the particular characteristic observable under different experimental conditions, the condition of light as wave, is also a property of one's interaction with light rather than a property of light itself. In short, whether particle or wave, what one sees is not objective reality but rather represents one's chosen method of interaction with reality. In quantum mechanics, interpretation becomes an ontological property to the extent that the chosen method of observation conditions the nature of what is observed.

To sum up, contemporary epistemology shows that there is an essential limitation on any attempt to explain reality in a way that is complete, objective, and unchanging. From Gödel comes the awareness that any axiomatic theory is inherently limited in the sense that it cannot offer a description of reality that is simultaneously complete and consistent, a limitation realized in the practice of the principles of Bohr and Heisenberg. Reality, insofar as it reflects the idea of essential indeterminacy, is incapable of algorithmic compression.

The evidence from science, reinforced by developments in linguistics, philosophy, and critical theory, points to a fundamental shift in the character of epistemology noted by Richard Rorty: from a foundationalist enterprise interested in separating certain knowledge from other forms of belief to a hermeneutic activity that sees knowledge as relative to specific contexts of interpretative understanding.[19] Knowledge can result, but its basis is contingent rather than privileged. What makes this epistemological theory of indeterminacy so pertinent to the present discussion of ethics and narrative is that it originated in sober scientific experiment rather than in mysticism or poetry, that physicists themselves now argue that the mechanistic viewpoint is inadequate to an understanding of both natural events and human action.[20] Of course, there are those who would criticize making what J. Robert Oppenheimer called "an immense evocative analogy" between quantum science and "situations of psychological and human experience," claiming that the essential ambiguity that quantum theory exposes is irrelevant to the macroscopic world of everyday affairs.[21] The point is not to dispute the existence in our lives of relationships such as cause and effect, however, but rather to show that classical determinism, once regarded as all-embracing and rigorous, is in fact inadequate to the task of cosmological speculation.

As science, classical determinism cannot account for anomalous phenomena, a flaw that in turn makes it impossible to extrapolate from classical determinism a "Newtonian" analogy to justify an ordered ethical stay against the perceived confusion of contemporary life. In contrast, the acceptance of the inherent presence of anomaly in quantum theory provides an epistemological base from which humans can extrapolate, if not perfect order, some ways of understanding indeterminacy in determinate ways and thus recover meaning in circumstances that otherwise appear to be contradictory and meaningless. For example, both Julia Kristeva, whose book *Essays in Semiotics* derives its ideology from Gödel's theorem, and Jacques Derrida, whose *Of Grammatology* draws terminology from quantum mechanics, provide powerful analyses of texts based on the claim that essential undecidability is a paradigm of all thinking.[22] For both authors, this process includes challenging the assumptions we make concerning the relationship of self and world. Drawing from the Newtonian conceptualization of reality as a collection of discrete entities keeps one focused on locating reality—and consequently truth—as the correct, totalizing metaphor of knowledge. In this context one assumes the existence of an objective map of reality, then seeks to establish location of reality, an action usually undertaken to insure the well-being of that most important of discrete entities humans conceptualize—the self. In contrast, drawing from the quantum conceptualization of reality means a shifting from location to vision as the basis for knowledge. In this context one sees that the "objective" map is not totalizing but provisional, no more than a Dymaxion or Mercator projection, ever subject to challenge, revision, or even replacement. Here the concern is not to find a secure vantage point within a fixed reality but rather to maintain a vision of alterity, the open-ended otherness of reality.

It should be noted here that I chose to omit Einstein from inclusion in this discussion of postmodern epistemology precisely because his rejection of essential indeterminacy and his desire to subsume all variables under a unified theoretical perspective amount to an unwillingness to challenge the Newtonian map. Einstein's theories of relativity substitute a different set of terms for the classical ones, leaving the basic epistemological structure of physics, particularly causal determinism, primarily unchanged. Quantum mechanics, in contrast, holds that essential indeterminacy is the fundamental principle underlying order. The results of the conflict between the two descriptions, most notably the resolution to the famous Einstein-Poldasky-Rosen (EPR) debate, would suggest that that the quantum vision is the more accurate.[23]

Because quantum science itself now explains reality as always including what physicist John Wheeler calls the "incontrovertible participator," the necessary presence of human subjectivity, the portrait of the scientist has changed: no longer the objective observer, a contemporary scientist is now involved in making decisions that are in many respects correlative with ethical

choice.[24] Accepting a pluriverse incapable of algorithmic compression, scientists accept knowledge without totalization. In so
doing, scientists also accept that acquisition of knowledge is not
only derivative and intuitive but negotiated, an interactive process requiring that they enact certain virtues, including an acceptance of the inherent diversity of experience, a toleration for
error, and especially a talent for metaphor, the willingness to
bend and adjust to new ways of thinking necessary when new
experience contravenes previous metaphors.

* * *

In arguing that Gaddis's novels exhibit an ethic of indeterminacy commensurate with the tenets of contemporary epistemology
outlined above, I am claiming that, as the epistemology of quantum mechanics shows we understand the world through our interactions with it, so too we should value our world through our
interactions with it. But if we are to believe that there can be a
morality congruent with this new epistemology, just what kind
of ethics can be extrapolated from the essential indeterminacy
and interaction of quantum mechanics to the realm of human
activity, and what form might it take?

For one thing, it would certainly mean forgoing the type of
moral legacy extrapolated from Newtonian epistemology, especially the concept of *Eidos*, the fundamental form that was accepted as the root cause of being and the basis of knowability.
As Joseph Fletcher explains in his book *Situation Ethics*, in this
context the connection between *is* and *ought* casts ethics as legalistic: a world in which prescriptive binding moral rules precede
experience and are revealed through it and whose validity is self-
warranted, determined by their formal consistency rather than
by the contingent ability to carry them out.

Nor could an ethics congruent with the new epistemology
espouse an antinomian ethic, where every moment of moral deci-

sion is made, as Sartre puts it, "when we have no excuses behind us and no justification before us."[25] One can admire the tough-minded and relentless existentialist pursuit to expose the bad faith of a world where much of the moral idiom serves as a mask concealing the arbitrary workings of power, but alienation itself finally must be regarded as a moral chimera. If the legalistic vision restricts the connection of *is* and *ought* to those self-warranted rules that exclude contingency, the antinomian rejects the *is/ought* connection altogether in its claim that the world is absurd. Yet the lament of the existential *I* rings hollow in the world Gaddis depicts, one where dehumanization and oppression grow increasingly unchecked. If originary ethics, in keeping with the basic meaning of *ethos*, refers to the world of the heaven and the earth, of the primordial and communal context in which mortals dwell, then an ethics of alienation not only offers no connection between *is* and *ought*, it offers no *ought* at all.

Gaddis offers as his ethic a timeless idea that receives a fresh dispensation from the new epistemology, an ethic of agapistic love. Unlike philia and Eros, *agapē*—a concept that appears in a variety of forms in Gaddis's novels—is neither emotional nor selective.[26] Instead, like the attitude of indeterminacy inherent in quantum mechanics, *agapē* represents a fundamental disposition of giving—nonreciprocally—in the face of any situation. The link between *is* and *ought* in this context is the idea that both to know the world and to act ethically in it one must set aside an absolute vantage point. This does not mean, however, that *agapē* ethics equate with the popularized version of situation ethics as "anything goes." Instead, as does contemporary epistemology, *agapē* ethics admit to a regulative standard: alterity, the world of the other. In *Inquiries into Truth and Interpretation*, Donald Davidson clarifies the conflation between epistemology and agapistic ethics when he writes: "If we want to understand, we must count others right in most situations."[27] In her essay "The Sublime and the

Good," Iris Murdoch further champions the connection between love and knowledge: "Love is the extremely difficult realization that something other than oneself is real. Love, and so art and morals, is the discovery of reality."[28]

Like the epistemology of quantum mechanics, agapistic ethics are a study in *Gelassenheit*, what Meister Eckhart defines as living "without why" and what Heidegger describes as an "openness to mystery," to be humble in the face of the irreducible otherness and contingency of experience.[29] As does the new epistemology, agapistic love has principles, but their power is regulative rather than constitutive, in experience rather than prior to it and always open to revision. In this morality, as in quantum physics, natural law is a concept undergirded by change rather than fixity, and virtuousness can be described as embracing the notion of competence in its biological context: an organism capable of successful transformation. In this context John Caputo's gloss of the fundamental agapistic tenet Gaddis cites on page 899 of *The Recognitions*—Augustine's "dilige, et quod vis fac" (that is, love and do what you will)—reminds us that, like the new epistemology, agapistic love means "coping with the flux": "Augustine meant that, if the heart is so filled with love that everything one does issues from love, then it is both unnecessary and impossible to spell out in detail just what it is one should or should not do. Indeed once one has to spell out obligations between lovers, the love is gone."[30] Analogous to the insight afforded by both Gödel's Theorem and Bohr's Principle of Complementarity, the notion of alterity in *agapē* can be understood as part of what ethical theorists refer to as a meta-ethical truth, a second-order description of the condition necessary to be ethical.[31]

But in offering several such variants of *agapē* love as the means for the redemption sought throughout his novels ("Damnation is life without love" asserts one character in *The Recognitions* [442], "the moral is the only way we know we are real" states another

[R 591], "the better of us keep one another in mind" offers Jack Gibbs [J R 290]), Gaddis does not proceed ignorant of the question posed by Reinhold Niebuhr: "How does an ethics of love speak to the exigencies of life in a fallen world?"[32] In seeking to use love as the means to circumvent the reduction of postmodern life to a Freudian dynamic of domination and submission, Gaddis also acknowledges the powerful challenge of Freud's claim that "there is no longer any place in present-day civilized life for a simple natural love between two human beings" by filling his novels with examples of just how contingent the possibility of enacting love is today.[33] Our world, Gaddis shows, is one of *agapē* agape: Augustine's quotation might serve as the ethical touchstone of *The Recognitions*, but Gaddis has that book's nefarious character, Anselm, remind us of the relativity of the deed, how difficult it is to love in the world. In attacking the artist Stanley's hagiographic preference for the Renaissance, Anselm reveals that agapistic love is radically contingent, existing only when one is willing to risk enacting it: "—Stanley, by Christ Stanley that's what it is, and you go around accusing people of refusing to humble themselves and submit to the love of Christ and you're the one, you're the one who refuses love, you're the one all the time who can't face it who can't face loving, and being loved right here, right in this lousy world, this god-damned world where you are right now, right . . . right now" (R 635).

The character Anselm's comments suggest two facets of *agapē* not yet discussed that together serve notice that for Gaddis the ethics of indeterminacy requires not only a second-order, meta-ethical description of right action but also a first-order application of ethical principle in a contingent world. One tenet of the first-order principle of *agapē*, analogous to Heisenberg's Principle of Indeterminacy, involves risk-taking as an integral part of love. As Harmon Smith describes it, in *agapē* risk finds meaning not in terms of the result of an action but as a constitutive part of that decision, a "risk *within* the decision making act,"[34] one where actively taking chances in the face of uncertainty becomes, as Gibbs states in *J R*, a necessary condition for any possibility of redemptive action: "Don't bring a God-damned thing to it can't take a goddamned thing away from it" (*J R* 605). Most pertinent to this discussion of Gaddis's postmodern ethics is that in such an ethics risk is not simply a conditional part of a situation that is ideally resolved once and for all. Instead, paralleling postmodern epistemology, risk is an essential component of agapistic ethics, reminding us that living ethically means remaining perpetually open to the mystery of the other.

The other tenet of Gaddis's first-order ethics of indeterminacy—the tenet of responsible suffering—also parallels Heisenberg's principle. In *The Recognitions* Gaddis makes much of the Pelagian heresy—the idea that man is responsible for his own salvation—and the problematic nature of achieving salvation in Anselm's "god-damned" world runs throughout his work. Accepting the essentially contingent nature of agapistic love requires a radical recasting of the relationship between self and the world, Gaddis's "courage to live without Absolutes" that is not unlike negative capability or the transvaluation of all values. Throughout his novels, however, Gaddis reminds us that most people are neither Keats's men of genius nor Nietzsche's *Ubermensch* but are at best what in his *Paris Review* interview Gaddis described *The Recognitions'* protagonist Wyatt as: men of talent.[35] In *J R* Jack Gibbs tells Edward Bast "genius does what it must talent does what it can," with no guarantee of success in this "god-damned world" (*J R* 117). For some, Gaddis tells us, talent equates with cupidity: "The important thing about [the character] J R is that he is *not* a genius. I wanted him to epitomize the amoral—which is to say simple, naked, cheerful greed."[36] In his work Gaddis shows that for the man of competence seeking to offset this amoral cheerful greed, the work of love involves not so much "do what you will" but rather the "dilige" aspect of Augustine's credo. In Gaddis's canon, *agapē* is not a feeling but a discipline in action, a bracketing of self so that one may assess and reassess where one's responsibilities lie in a world whose map is ever subject to change. For men of talent to maintain such competence requires that one enact the principle of living deliberately as the willingness to suffer the responsibility of revising the map without resorting to what Nietzsche defined as *ressentiment*, the moralizing of suffering.[37] To endure suffering is to embrace the virtue Gaddis alludes to in *The Recognitions* as "What Wotan taught his son. . . . The power of doing without happiness" (*R* 552). Although unacknowledged by Gaddis, these lines also allude to Eliot's comment in "The Dry Salvages":

> We had the experience but missed the meaning,
> And approach to the meaning restores the experience
> In a different form, beyond any meaning
> We can assign to happiness.

In contrast, to refeel the effect of suffering by necessarily holding some agent morally responsible for it is to shift the focus from action to complaint, embracing the twin ills of convention and neurosis, the enemies of agapistic love: neither pictures virtue as concerned with anything real outside the self; both tend toward solipsism by identifying the sufferer as the very agent he seeks to blame.

The fact that most of Gaddis's characters retreat to neurosis and convention makes it clear that suffering Wotan's secret is no easy task. If acknowledging alterity is the moral obligation required by *agapē*, then taking risks and suffering responsibly are acts of supererogation beyond the capacities of most people. The wisdom of Tolstoy's *Kingdom of God* (*The Kingdom of God Is within You: or, Christianity Not as a Mystical Teaching but as a New*

Concept of Life) is an implicit rallying point for correct action in Gaddis's fiction (R 442), but by also alluding to lines from Tolstoy's *Redemption*, Gaddis reminds readers that most men of talent who seek redemption share Fedya's problem: there is "something terribly lacking between what I felt and what I could do" (R 606, J R 248).[38] In Gaddis's second novel, *agapē* is offset by the fact that in Gibbs's "god-damned world" of corporate America, the virtues of love are seen as tax write-offs (J R 212) or else renounced altogether (J R 37). If we cannot, as Jack Gibbs reminds readers in J R, "escape" our "God-damned Protestant ethic" but instead "have to redeem it" (J R 477), by the time Gaddis writes *Carpenter's Gothic* the sleaze and corruption of "having business with the Bible" give fresh currency to Nietzsche's aphorism that Christ may well have been the only Christian: "The Christian principle of love: in the end it wants to be PAID well."[39] In Gaddis's third and darkest novel, the ethic to be redeemed is Weberian late capitalist. *Carpenter's Gothic* offers up no quotation concerning love, for in this novel love is excarnated, trivialized to a disembodied commodity sold by fundamentalists and others "having business with the Bible." What results, *Carpenter's Gothic* repeatedly specifies, is a world of selfish stupidity: what Gaddis, in referring to Schiller in J R, describes as the most pernicious enemy of Wotan's secret: "With Stupidity the Gods themselves struggle in vain" (J R 189).[40] In *Carpenter's Gothic* Gaddis several times reminds readers that there is "a fine line between the truth and what really happened" (C's G 130, 136, 191, 193, 240), and in terms of postmodern ethics the novel shows that although the preached "truth" might remain the humane values of Christ, "what really happened" is the transformation of Christ to kitsch: a commodity marked by the ersatz, vicarious, faked experience and sanctioned by a populace that in general remains crass and obtuse. One might justifiably rail, as does humanist McCandless in *Carpenter's Gothic*, against the "values" of this culture "verging ever closer to chance,"[41] but Gaddis reminds us that in a society lacking stable human values, seeking conventional humanist solutions leads to total skepticism, to total expediency, or in the case of McCandless, to both.

But if Gaddis's novels show an increasingly dark resolution to the ethical quest to redeem the Protestant ethic, an inability to live deliberately when this requires the supererogatory enactment of the vision of agapistic alterity in a world clearly without absolutes, I believe his point is to show the failure of love as a denial of our true situation rather than an acknowledgment of it. This claim may sound strange given the fact that whatever voices in the novel that do espouse such wisdom are largely drowned out by the din of venality that pervades Gaddis's novels. But even if the characters' actions did confirm the truth of agapistic love as an ethical force, this would limit the novels to being no more than another version of what Jeffrey Stout calls "moral *bricolage*" or Jefferey Minson describes as "eccentricity in ethical reasoning": strong and articulate theories about how moral principles could become part of the postmodern scene with little or no direction concerning just how to put these theories into practice.[42] Gaddis, in contrast, provides clarification for how one might practice such an ethic, not simply in what he says but also in how he says it. In this context Gaddis provides a warrant for believing that agapistic ethics apply to postmodern experience by using language in a necessarily peculiar way—a way that reflects the special status that contemporary epistemology confers on the ideas of complementarity and indeterminacy as regulative guides to the essential risk-taking action of *agapē* in a contingent world.

Through this use of language Gaddis recasts the role of the reader. No longer simply a detached observer, the reader becomes what Gaddis has called a "collaborator," one who regards the text as a blueprint for meaning whose actualization emerges from actions the collaborative reader chooses to perform.[43] By confronting the reader with an essentially indeterminate text, Gaddis moves the reader from an abstract to a concrete, experiential grasp of his "true situation," of how alterity, risk-taking, and suffering are all necessary to have even a possibility of recovering meaning from such conditions. Because the novels' language reflects the features of postmodern epistemological explanation, readers discover this method as they work out the linguistic perplexities they encounter; the experience of how to read the text, how to formulate literary meaning, also shows them potentially how to read the ineluctably anomalous postmodern world and recover meaning in it. In this sense Gaddis requires that his reader become a man of competence, attesting to the power and difficulty of Wotan's secret by diligently stitching together texts that refuse the happiness of lyrical closure.[44]

What emerges from this discussion is the experience of an essentially problematic ethic: a vision of alterity reached through exercising the virtues of risk-taking and suffering, undergirded by the notion of essential transformation. For Gaddis, the real world is one which, as Derrida puts it, exposes the common habitation of good and evil—*agapē* and agape—in the postmodern landscape: "There is no ethics without the presence of the other, but also, and consequently, without absence, dissimulation, detour, difference, writing. The arche-writing is the origin of morality as of immorality."[45] Through the form of his novels Gaddis reminds his reader that it is the imperative of the call to moral action plus the indicative agapistic acting that might allow at least a provisional normative redeeming of the postmodern Protestant ethic.

*   *   *

Actually preserving traces of real experience of the new epistemology and agapistic ethics within the folds of nonsensuous mimetic narrative is no mean feat, however, for the difficulty of writing a novel whose language embodies this vision is not the absence of desire. The problem is, rather, that the conventional logic of our language is itself mechanistic and apparently cannot represent indeterminacy and complementarity except as noncommunicative chaos: a meaningless condition that renders communication illusory. As Roland Barthes explains: "Language as sentence, period and paragraph, superimposes on these discontinuous categories existing at the level of discourse the appearance of discourse. Because no matter how discontinuous language itself may appear, its structure is so well established in the experience of each man that he grasps discourse as a continuous reality—the obligatory rubric of the completed sentence."[46]

As both Katherine Hayles in *The Cosmic Web* and Robert Nadeau in *Readings from the New Book of Nature* point out, the issue of how to incorporate the vision afforded by quantum physics in narrative form, the way to affirm meaning in the face of essential anomaly, requires methods not yet developed by most postmodern writers.[47] Hayles, quoting Pynchon in *Gravity's Rainbow*, describes the problem as follows: "Our relation to the field [her cynosure for postmodern epistemology] of the cosmos is a 'tremendous and secret function' whose meaning finally cannot be spoken," a sentiment echoed by Nadeau when he describes the "absence of the yet to be imagined conventions in the novel congruent with the new metaphysic."[48]

The development of such methods certainly is a formidable task, because it involves answering the fundamental question posed by Heidegger, "whether the nature of Western Language is in itself marked with an exclusive brand of metaphysics, and thus marked permanently by onto-theo-logic, or whether this same language offers other possibilities of utterance."[49]

Once again the epistemology of quantum physics provides a useful gloss. In acknowledging such limits in the empirical realm, quantum theory further undercuts the fundamental premise of Newtonian scientific explanation: that no theory is valid unless

every perceived element in the real world has a definite counterpart in the theory used to describe the world. In quantum theory
this one-to-one correspondence no longer applies. Because quantum theory can only predict probabilities, individual events are
chance happenings that have no corresponding theoretical element. Put another way, quantum theory forgoes explanation in
terms of classical scientific language because it acknowledges that
understanding phenomena cannot occur through the use of theoretical symbols alone. In the course of the development of quantum theory, a crucial understanding emerged: the theory was
difficult to explain not because it was complicated but because the
words used to communicate it were not adequate for explaining
quantum phenomena. In writing about the formulation of these
theories at the Solvay Conference in Brussels in 1927, Heisenberg
described the problem this way: "The real difficulty behind the
many controversies was the fact that no language existed in which
one could speak consistently about the new situation. The ordi-
nary language of science was based upon old concepts of space
and time, and this language offered the only unambiguous means
of communication. Yet the experiments [in quantum theory]
showed that the old concepts could not be applied everywhere."[50]

To rely on symbols is to ignore Bohr's oft-repeated statement
that we are "suspended in language," that any linguistic description is necessarily partial insofar as the rules governing the forma-
tion of the concept (e.g., particle / wave) do not bind experience
itself.[51] True understanding does not depend on the way we think
of things but on the ways we participate in the experience of
them.

The need to experience something to understand it is not new.
Prior to current explanations of physics, however, the epistemological status of experience was secondary, at best a stage to a
real understanding of universals. Experience itself was not ultimate; the inherent paradoxes and errors of the senses created a

preference for first principles and rational certainty over mere empiric generalizations as the source of truth. With the advent of postmodern epistemology, however, experience assumes an ontological dimension insofar as the choices and measurements of the participant in an experiment help constitute the nature of the phenomenon observed.

The inference from such acceptance of the irreducible imprecision of scientific principles is not that the systematic search for understanding be abandoned. Rather, it is that understanding is reached through experience as much as through theory. When Bohr and Heisenberg faced the conceptual paradoxes of their experiments, their acceptance of the role experience plays in understanding allowed them to formulate theories that, although incomplete by traditional standards, explained previously inexplicable phenomena. Perhaps the most startling example of this acceptance concerns Heisenberg's radical redefinition of mathematical symbols as words, as placeholders whose presence, while violating not only orthodox mathematics but also common-sense intuition, allowed the formulation of matrix mechanics, a breakthrough not permissible in antecedent formulations.[52] In general, the linguistic, metaphoric descriptions of events in quantum physics appear to be regulative rather than constitutive: not an attempt to communicate accurately and completely an experience itself but rather to provide guidelines for how someone else can have that same experience.

To be suspended in language, then, does not mean that no progress can be made. Instead, progress is made not by underplaying the limitations of a viewpoint but by systematically exploiting them. As Bohr explained, "The development of physics has taught us that . . . even the most elementary concepts . . . [are] based on assumptions initially unnoticed." By examining carefully these concepts, scientists "obtain a classification of more extended domains of experience. These more extended domains are in turn underlaid by other concepts containing unrecognized presuppositions, the examination of which will in turn lead to a more general description."[53] In sum, quantum science solved the onto-theo-logic problem by changing the basic premise of language so that by definition it included a nonsymbolic experiential component, showing how language was capable of providing other possibilities of utterance when it was understood as a linking of symbol and experience.

William Gaddis has also found other possibilities of utterance by employing narrative methods that extend past the onto-theo-logic of essential structure. In reading Gaddis this way, I mean to show how the idea of language as a linking of symbol and experience put forth by quantum physics is also the informing principle of his works by incorporating into the novels' respective modes of discourse the same conditions imposed on meaning and value by the new epistemology.

To accomplish this, Gaddis creates conditions for the reader that require him to implement the values of the ethics of indeterminacy. First, Gaddis shows that essential structure is an artificial condition imposed by language rather than a natural condition. In both *The Recognitions* and *J R* Gaddis presents this in two ways. First, he attacks the premise of a universal, rational structure by writing novels wherein rival systems of order conflict but never resolve, never reach a condition of closure. Because of their encyclopedic nature, both novels constantly bombard the reader with the doctrines of various "isms"—mythic, religious, scientific, political, literary, and economic. Yet the novels do not reflect the superiority of any one system; instead, the reader is left with the impression that no single system can lay claim to the truth. To reinforce this concern with the fraudulence of essential structure, Gaddis sets this demonstration in a narrative form that dramatizes it. Through a variety of techniques, Gaddis creates the same conditions for readers that he does for the characters inside them:

no matter how many conceptual strands of meaning readers pick up, they are always left with important information that cannot be reconciled within a single, consistent interpretation. Employing what Benjamin—and more recently Derrida—explained as collage, or transfer of material from one context to another, I argue that Gaddis creates in his narratives what Derrida describes as a a "double reading": "the fragment perceived in relation to its text of origin; that of the same fragment as incorporated into a new whole, a different totality. The trick of collage consists also of never entirely suppressing the alterity of these elements reunited in a temporary composition."[54]

For Benjamin this type of work left open the possibility of emancipation: freeing art from the realm of shopworn ideas and cathartic experiences to one of critical cultural argument. The task of the artist in such a climate is to present art as a product, something that requires the same collaborative activity on the part of the reader mentioned by Gaddis. As Benjamin writes, "A writer's production must have the character of a model: it must be able to instruct other writers in their production and secondly, it must be able to place an improved apparatus at their disposal. The apparatus will be better the more consumers it brings into contact with the production process—in short the more readers or spectators it turns into collaborators."[55]

Benjamin's concept of a collaborator, an active agent of transformation, is reinforced when one considers Benjamin's distinction between the nature of knowledge and the nature of truth, a distinction made manifest in terms of how readers must transform the material presented to them. Benjamin believed knowledge was amenable to systematic statement and theory, a style that required no active participation on the part of the reader. Truth, in contrast, rejected a sequence of ordered presentation, requiring of the reader instead a disjunctive, fragmented style with which the reader, as Benjamin implied, must stop and restart

with every sentence.[56] Benjamin called this technique of presenting the truth *plumpes denken* (crude thought), the utilization
of thought fragments whose power was "not the strength to preserve but to cleanse, to tear out of context, to destroy the illusion
of history."[57] Benjamin made extensive use of these thought fragments, particularly quotations, but not as conventional illustra-
tions for the text. Instead, his intention was to create a text
made up entirely of fragments, an intention Theodor Adorno
described as "the attempt to abandon all apparent construction
and to leave [the text's] significance to emerge solely out of the
shock-like montage of the material."[58] The intent, made clear
by Benjamin, was to disrupt: "Quotations in my works are like
robbers by the roadside who make an armed attack and relieve the
idler of his convictions."[59] Benjamin also stressed the necessary
obliquity of these fragments, stating that "the value of the fragments of thought is all the greater the less their direct relationship
to the underlying idea."[60] The key to understanding does not lie
in reading that which is immediately given but instead in being
able in effect to read what was never written.[61] The reader breaks
into "the discontinuous structure of the world to reveal from
behind the piles of refuse . . . small material particles that indicate
what is essential."[62] This approach, as Benjamin describes in "The
Destructive Character," requires that one break up the world and
its wish-symbols. But "he reduces what exists to ruins, not in
order to create ruins, but in order to find the way that leads
through them."[63]

Although Gaddis never specifically refers to Benjamin in his
novels, the fact that both men focus on fragmentation, quotation,
and reader participation in remarkably similar ways gives credence
to what both Barthes and Kristeva suggest is the condition of
"anonymous intertextuality."[64] These general similarities, together with what I will argue in chapter 3 are specific albeit
oblique references to Benjamin in *J R*, suggest that Benjamin is

to Gaddis what God is to Kafka or, more appropriately, what Husserl is to Beckett—a significant influence that remains at the level of an unnamable.[65]

In effect enacting Bohr's theory of complementarity and Gödel's incompleteness theorem simultaneously, what results from this collage technique present in Gaddis's work is the textual equivalent of the reader's moral obligation: acknowledgment of the validity of the concept of alterity, the second-order, meta-ethical component of *agapē*. This is the recognition that any conceptual understanding is partial and inadequate by itself, that complete explanation is always complementary in that such explanations admit the existence of other, mutually exclusive interpretations.

Although necessary, the deconstructive impulse to expose the fraudulence of an a priori structure is by itself insufficient to clarify how to live deliberately, to provide a sense of just how postmodern agapistic ethics might function. For that to occur, readers must not only be exposed to the complementary nature of understanding: they must also learn how it is possible to recover meaning in an indeterminate world.

To accomplish this recognition, Gaddis uses narrative techniques that in effect enact Heisenberg's Principle of Indeterminacy, which says the choices observers make help constitute the reality they perceive. Applied to narrative, this concept means that the reader becomes an active party in the construction of the narrative, moving from the meta-ethical awareness to applied ethical action to recover meaning from the novels. In both *The Recognitions* and *J R*, Gaddis enforces this move by using parabolic allusion. Similar in nature to Benjamin's oblique thought fragments, these allusions' connections to the text are sufficiently indirect that to apply them to the text readers are required to transfer Gaddis's invention theory to their own reading. Enacting in effect an act of supererogatory textual "virtue," the reader is required to move beyond simply interpreting juxtaposed fragments already present to become what both Gaddis and Benjamin mean by a collaborator, a reader who actively superimposes fragments brought to the text in essence to read what was never written. In *J R*, Gaddis takes this narrative enactment of indeterminacy one step further by writing a 726-page novel that consists entirely of dialogue. In so doing, Gaddis insures that the reader cannot perceive the narrative as a determinant object that can be objec-tively observed. Instead, this technique requires that the reader participate in a dialogue with the text, participating experientially as well as conceptually in the construction of meaning, enacting the risk and responsible suffering that make up the first-order virtues of *agapē*. In *Carpenter's Gothic* Gaddis both modifies and extends these techniques by adding factual information that resists aesthetic closure, reminding the reader that the tendency to methodize indeterminacy falsifies the understanding of essential indeterminacy: all tropes, fragmentary or not, can never replicate reality; they can only lead one to the experience of it.

In *Ecce Homo 3* Nietzsche defines the perfect reader as "a monster of courage and curiosity, moreover supple, cunning cau-tious, a born adventurer and discoverer," a definition equally applicable to the supererogatory reader demanded by Gaddis's narratives. Of course, Gaddis's novels cannot force acceptance of his vision: instead of choosing to suffer the difficulties of reading narratives that mirror a world without absolutes, the reader could respond egoistically or, like Didi and Gogo, not respond at all. Nevertheless, Gaddis's texts make substantive claims about what is worthwhile and how one should live, claims whose status is validated by the conditions for meaning the texts present. Having set down the basic outline of Gaddis's narrative strategy, what remains is to explore the logic of his materials.

2 . . . . .
The Recognitions

Fallor Ergo Sum. (For if I am deceived, I am.)
—*St. Augustine, City of God*

• • • A first reading of *The Recognitions* leaves one with the clear impression that the novel is a mythology manual, a 956-page dramatization of almost every myth, ritual, and archetype present in the novel's acknowledged sourcebooks: *The Golden Bough, The White Goddess,* and *The Integration of the Personality.*[1] Understood in this fashion, the correct method of critical analysis seems self-evident: one looks up all the allusions, then links them to some ur-myth, rite de passage, or quest to show how Gaddis reminds us once more of the importance of what T. S. Eliot called the "mythical method," "the continuous parallel between contemporaneity and antiquity" that enables writers and readers to give "a shape and a significance to the immense panorama of futility and anarchy which is contemporary history."[2] If the world in general has lost touch with the primordial forces of life, literate people can regain historical consciousness by reading "big books" like *The Recognitions* that are chock-full of mythic fragments that can shore up the ruins of the demythologized landscape.

Within the novel itself, the mythic quests of identity and consubstantiality seem to provide the scaffolding for the life of the novel's protagonist, the artist/priest Wyatt Gwyon. The author divides the novel, spanning a period of thirty-one years from 1919 to 1950, into three main sections. The first chronicles the events surrounding the death of Wyatt's mother, Camilla, and his subsequent upbringing in a household "saturated with priesthood" (R 373). The remainder of this section details the conflicting values that Wyatt is exposed to: a rigid Puritanism embodied by his Aunt May and a heretical paganism embodied by his father, a Protestant minister who has given up the preaching of Christianity in favor of pagan cults, especially the Mithraic worship of the sun.

The book's second section traces the events of Wyatt's quest once he renounces the priesthood to become an artist who seeks the genuine amid the fraud and counterfeit of the art world as portrayed in this novel. It is ironic, however, that Wyatt's scruples are quickly put to ill use. Specifically, Wyatt becomes involved in an art-forging scheme in which his considerable talent for copying is used to make faithful imitations of the works of old masters. The works are sold at auctions as originals, exposed as frauds by the spoiled priest turned art critic Basil Valentine, then "authenticated" as originals by the same deceptive critic, who, now persuaded by their originality, certifies their value to a gullible public.

The novel's final section follows Wyatt to Spain, where, after renouncing the art scheme, he retreats to a monastery to "restore" old masters by scraping the overlap of originals back to the *prima materia* of the white canvas. The novel concludes unresolved, with Wyatt, now called Stephen Asche, conflating his martyr and salvation quests by fathering a child with a prostitute and adopting a Thoreau-like posture "to simplify" (900), and the epilogue of the novel serves as a fifty-six-page apocalyptic coda: assassinations, suicide, death from disease, acts of theft and counterfeit, and a frontal lobotomy prefigure the collapse of a Spanish church described in the last lines of the book.

Despite some interesting and comic twists in this portrayal, *The Recognitions* seems to offer simply another version of the well-worn observation that in a venal and fragmented world humans must return to their origins to recover their identity. Although the panorama of the novel is certainly anarchic and although a major concern of its characters is finding some form of redemptive order within such a world, Gaddis does not use his mythic allusions to help his characters and readers find *the* way. Instead of juxtaposing various myths to reveal some otherwise hidden unconditioned ground of being, Gaddis juxtaposes myth in a manner similar to Benjamin's disruptive "thought fragments" to reveal that there is no warrant for belief in such a ground and that true recognition means in part understanding that any system of meaning claiming such a warrant is counterfeit. In *The Recognitions* Gaddis enacts Frazer's definition of myth as "mistaken explanations of phenomena," a language of symbolic forms that when interposed between humans and the outside world arbitrarily imposes order on the world so that humans might apprehend it.[3] Gaddis extends Frazer's critique of ancient myth to include modern science, institutionalized religion, and art, because they too lay claim to a special understanding of the truth and to the means of reaching it.

Read from this perspective, *The Recognitions* demonstrates the essential alterity of the world, the meta-ethical virtue of agapistic ethics, by forcing the reader to acknowledge and accept the inherent ambiguity limiting any systematized approach to understanding. Despite the absolutist claims of myths, ours is a world without absolutes.

The novel enacts this demonstration in two ways. Within the book, the reader finds three conflicting mythic systems of order: Christianity, technological science, and "alchemical" art. At first, the resolution of the conflict appears to mirror the aesthetic preference common in twentieth-century narrative, because Gaddis uses alchemical art to expose the ways in which Christianity and science are counterfeit means of understanding. If the Protestant ethic needs redeeming, then art, whose context in this novel is the redemptive power of alchemy, certainly can provide the means of living deliberately. Ultimately, however, Gaddis rejects the aesthetic solution as well, for he turns alchemical art in on itself to demonstrate that it too is counterfeit insofar as it claims to be the true way of reaching understanding.

Gaddis not only critiques the myth of essential structure within the novel; he enacts its truth by setting this critique in a narrative that dramatizes it. *The Recognitions* at once invites and resists the reader's attempts to organize its 956 pages of allusions, constantly tempting him to use Eliot's mythical method to seek out extensive patterns of interlocking motifs hidden beneath the chaotic narrative surface of the novel. The novel intractably resists formulation, however, frustrating such efforts by means of a variety of techniques that undercut these patterns. The readers of *The Recognitions*, like the characters inside it, come to realize that singular solutions are impossible, that there is no true ur-myth, no philosopher's stone whose true nature will be revealed by applying the right mix of interpretation. The only answer to the riddle of meaning posed by the fragmented form of the novel is that there is always more than one right answer to riddles. All singular interpretations, artistic or otherwise, are frauds; all such interpreters, be they characters or readers, are forgers.

Alchemy, a concept that at first appears to be the preferred method of achieving redemption, is introduced by the book's title, taken from a work that is, as the character Basil Valentine indicates, the probable source of the Faust legend: "The what? *The Recognitions*? No, it's Clement of *Rome*. Mostly talk, talk, talk. The young man's deepest concern is for the immortality of his soul, he goes to Egypt to find magicians and learn their secrets. It's been referred to as the first Christian novel. What? Yes, it's really the beginning of the whole Faust legend" (373).

Bereft of the value of traditional myths of redemption, both pagan and Christian, the novel's protagonist, Wyatt, takes on the characteristics of the Faustian man in Spengler's Faustian age, the artist / magician searching for salvation.[4] The Faustian / alchemical motif introduced by the title is reinforced by the graphic presentation, on the frontispiece of the original edition, of the *ouroborous*, the alchemical dragon devouring its own tail. These introductory references point to a concept that echoes at once the relationship between good and evil, man's revolt against limitations and the concomitant thirst for knowledge associated with closure, and the radical disparity between theoretical sublimity and actual misery in human existence: in short, a concept that highlights Gaddis's concern with questions of value in an epistemological context.

Because alchemy plays such a significant role in understanding the notion of artistic redemption described in *The Recognitions*, an explanation of some of alchemy's more basic tenets is in order. As Jung's pioneering work on the subject suggests, the true aims of alchemy were not the popularized follies of wizened magicians transmuting lead into gold but the reconciliation of opposites and the redemption of matter.[5] According to Jung, alchemy states that there is an essential if hidden connection of the microcosmos and the macrocosmos, an integration that Joyce adroitly parodies in *Finnegans Wake* as "the tasks above are like the flasks below" and that Gaddis echoes in Reverend Gwyon's hiding a flask of schnapps in a hollowed-out copy of *The Dark Night of the Soul* (23). Despite the burlesque treatment, however, both Joyce's and Gaddis's comments also illustrate a basic tenet of the hermetic art: that the base is never transfigured but instead remains co-present with the high. As Otto, echoing Wyatt, explains to Esther early in the novel, matter and redemption are inextricable: "Yes, but I mean, today we were talking about alchemy, and the mysteries about the redemption of matter and that it wasn't just making gold, trying to make real gold, but that matter. . . . Matter, he said was a luxury, was our great luxury, and that matter, I mean redemption" (129). It is ironic that Otto never understands the true import of what he says. His comments, however, allude to the second important tenet of alchemy, its dual physical and spiritual nature, frequently referred to as exoteric and esoteric alchemy.

Exoteric alchemy concerns itself with the purely physical and "miraculous" act of transforming a base metal into gold. The exoteric process takes place in a laboratory with the use of heated ovens and chemicals, which were believed to transmute the metal, effecting a change from a base state to a purified one. Because this process promised both wealth and power, the transformation primarily concerns greed and control and can involve that extreme extension of the rational mind so often characterized as the Faustian desire to transcend all limits through the logos and to exalt the primacy of the self.[6]

Scholarship on the subject, however, suggests that the real and fecund purposes of alchemy did not rest in the scientific laboratory.[7] Instead, the power of alchemy is directed from the physical to the spiritual, with the concept of esoteric transformation describing humanity's movement toward spiritual perfection. This transformation of the base (or sinful) to gold (or spiritual) can represent the end of a cosmic and spiritual process, at the same time serving as the re-creation and restoration of the original divine state of being. The true laboratory of the esoteric alchemists, then, is not the scientific workshop but the laboratory of the soul, where the ultimate goal was the spiritual transformation of humans to their highest and most perfect state, a state always dormant within each person.

The catalyst in the equation between the chemical process and humans' souls is the imagination, what the fifteenth-century alchemist Paracelsus termed the *archeus*. For Paracelsus, the imagination was the most important human faculty, enabling people either to achieve heavenly unity or to unleash destructive powers.[8] Paracelsus maintained that the *archeus* was the "active principle and vector of life," was connected with the rational while also a part of the universal soul, an emanation of the divine and supernatural. Through the *archeus*, "something reserved to the individual and at the same time shared by every object of nature, man could recreate and purify himself."[9] Esoteric alchemy, then, is the art of releasing the hidden, purifying the base, and transforming man to the highest state of being, specifically through the power of the imagination.

In *The Recognitions*, alchemy, expanded to include the transformational power of Wyatt's artistic imagination, maintains this link between low and high, between physical and spiritual, and in so doing appears preferable to rival systems, specifically science and religion, as a myth of redemption, an organized means of recovering a unified sense of purpose amid the chaos, venality, and malevolence portrayed in *The Recognitions*. Within the novel's Spenglerian world, where religion is depicted as little more than "a disciplined superstition" (825), Gaddis has Wyatt seek redemption in the powers of art. As Gaddis states in his notes, "the process of art is the artist's working out of his own redemption," and in *The Recognitions* the nature of art is closely aligned with alchemy.[10] Wyatt himself quotes the alchemical dictum "Amor Perfectissmus," or most perfect love (392), as his credo, and throughout the novel he is obsessed with maintaining the purity of his material, which, as Jung points out, was a fundamental tenet in alchemy.[11] The most important link between art and alchemy in this novel, however, concerns the quest for authenticity. Wyatt's quest, like that of his alchemical counterparts, concerns the transformational recognitions demanded in the title: the esoteric "gold" of truth hidden beneath the "base" values of a contemporary society that embraces the exoteric myths of science and religion. Throughout the novel, Gaddis acknowledges this hierarchy of myth, demonstrating how Wyatt's esoteric art surpasses both science and religion as a means of providing man with order, purpose, and meaning.

As the following passage indicates, Gaddis at first seems to regard alchemy as inferior to chemistry, its more sober scientific successor: "And once chemistry had established itself as true and legitimate son and heir, alchemy was turned out like a drunken parent, to stagger away, babbling phantasies to fewer and fewer ears, to less and less impressive derelicts of loneliness while the child grew up serious, dignified and eminently pleased with its own limitations to indulge that parental memory with no doubt but that it had found what the old fool and his cronies were after all the time" (132).

The superiority of "sober" chemistry, however, is radically undercut by several passages that demonstrate how much science both avoids and perverts life. In *The Recognitions* Gaddis portrays science as technology run amok: it can extend life quantitatively but not qualitatively, can skewer dead babies on electrodes but cannot "rescue our cadavers from the worms of the grave" (414), and can cut "open Caruso's throat when he died to see what made him sing" (623). What is most grotesque about such applications of science, however, is that they illustrate the basic premise of science and of our technological age, what Gaddis refers to variously as "the modernism heresy" (178) and "the self-sufficiency of fragments": "That's where the curse is, fragments that don't belong to anything. Separately they don't mean anything, but it's almost impossible to pull them together into a whole" (616). If science is more concerned with dissection than with integration, Gaddis seems to be saying, then how can science provide true understanding?

Gaddis's answer, of course, is that science cannot, and in contrast to a science he calls "the enlightenment of total materialism" (132) Gaddis offers the progressive revelation of alchemy, "that doctrine which finds man incapable of receiving truth all of a lump, but offers it to him only in a series of fragments, any one of which, standing by itself, might be disproven by someone unable to admit that he is, eventually, after the same thing" (132). Alchemy is thus the opposite of science, which according to Gaddis offers only self-contained "lumps" of information that have abstracted, reduced, and distorted experience.

The perceived superiority of alchemy as the preferred means of recovering unity and purpose is further reinforced when it is compared to its other rival redemptive mode in this novel, Christianity. In *The Recognitions*, Christianity is not portrayed as a religion embodying the beliefs of a Saint Francis embracing the humanistic spirits of Renaissance artists. As he did with science, Gaddis shuns historical objectivity in his portrayal of Christianity to clarify how its institutional nature has perverted its humanistic tendencies. Valentine defines this tendency when he contrasts the success of Christianity to the failure of its greatest rival, Mithraism: "Come along, dear fellow, I'll tell you why Mithraism failed, the greatest rival Christianity ever had. It failed because it lacked central authority" (553). When the church fathers equated Christ and the Logos, Gaddis seems to be saying, they replaced immanence and its concomitant syncretism and mysteries with a transcendence that appeared rational, controlled, and authoritative.[12] For Gaddis, however, what is most significant about institutionalized Christianity is what it lacks: a concern for the physical. Gaddis illustrates this deficiency in his portrait of an early church father, Origen. This disciple of Clement became so enamored of the ninth chapter of Matthew that "he castrated himself so that he might repeat the *hoc est corpus meum, Dominus*, without the distracting interference of the flesh" (103). What results from acts such as these, Gaddis suggests, is a celebration of transcendent values at the expense of the physical, a denial of life that he believes continues to inform Christianity: "So well had Origen succeeded in sowing his field without a seed, that the conspiracy, conceived in light, born bred in darkness and harassed to maturity in dubious death and rapturous martyrdom continued. *Miserere nobis* said the mitered lips. *Vae victis*, the statistical heart" (103).

By focusing on Christianity as a conspiracy, Gaddis's aim seems clear: to expose Christianity's perceived distortions of substance and salvation. As Gaddis tells the reader, "Tragedy was forsworn in the ritual denial of the ripe knowledge that we are drawing away from one another, or to others, or to God" (103). Christianity lacks, in other words, what science also lacks in comparison with alchemy—a syncretic transformational process that acknowledges the place of the physical and the flawed and seeks to transform them rather than simply deny them significance or destroy them altogether. Although Wyatt exclaims that "Charity's the challenge" (383), it is significant that Gaddis ascribes this virtue, as well as hope and faith, to another character, Pivner. The lonely everyman of the novel, Pivner's adherence to transformational virtue is rendered anomalous by a society that has institutionalized virtue: "What was this anomaly in him, that still told him that the human voice is to be listened to? the printed word to be read? What was this expectant look, if it was not hope? this attentive weariness, if it was not faith? this bewildered failure to damn, if it was not charity?" (502). The fact that Pivner winds up lobotomized is Gaddis's chilling reminder that, for commoners, seeking to enact the transformational virtues of Christianity has been reduced to a mindless activity, a reduction at least in part sanctioned by institutionalized Christianity's conspiratorial focus on power and control.

The contrast between Christianity and alchemy is further clarified by Jung's testimony on the latter. When Jung describes alchemy's concern for the mysteries of living that religion has forsworn, he explains that alchemy compensates for Christianity's inability to synthesize, to reconcile opposites: "The point is that alchemy is rather like an undercurrent to the Christianity that ruled the surface. It is to this surface as the dream is to the consciousness, and just as the dream compensates the conflicts of the conscious mind, so alchemy endeavors to fill in the gray area left open by the Christian tension of opposites."[13] But alchemy is not limited to a compensatory dream for Jung: he further asserts that alchemy transcends Christianity in the active status alchemy accords individuals in their quests: "Man [in alchemy] is both the redeemed and the redeemer. The first formulation is Christian, the second alchemical. In the first case man attributes the need of redemption to himself and leaves the work of redemption . . . to the autonomous divine figure; in the latter case man takes upon himself the duty of carrying out the redeeming opus."[14] In *The Recognitions* the superiority of alchemy to both science and Christianity is clear. Science dissects and destroys substance; Christianity determines the nature of substance through rhetoric at the Council of Nicea; alchemy explores, touches, and finally transforms substance through discovery, a process that requires active participation by the individual. In this novel, science and Christianity are indeed examples of what Paul Tillich called "a broken myth," a societal structure devoid of human significance. In *The Recognitions*, the fractures in these myths are nowhere more evident than in the rash of suicides, murders, lobotomies, dismemberments, and bestial acts that occur during the five hundred pages that describe Christmas week. For Gaddis, Christ's day has failed.

Despite its encyclopedic catalog of mythic allusions, then, it seems clear that Gaddis did not intend *The Recognitions* to be understood as an epic. When Homer, Virgil, and Milton wrote their works, they provided their contemporaries with a vivid image of the past, generating a mythical identity that in turn pointed to the possibility of a unified present society. In *The Recognitions*, however, Gaddis thwarts the notion of the past constructively informing the present, offering instead a chaotic present that articulates only the irrelevance and mendacity of past myths.

In *The Recognitions*, for example, the reader finds a variety of allusions to atonement, both Christian and pagan, but their efficacy is undercut by trivializing their origins. To see this, one need only contrast the epigraph from Irenaeus, the second-century defender of Orthodox Christianity, with the title, taken from the Ebionate heretic Clement, to catch Gaddis's mock-epical attitude toward all doctrine. From Father Eulalio, "a thriving lunatic of eight-six who was castigating himself for unchristian pride at having all the vowels in his name" (10), to the collapse of the church at the end of the novel, Gaddis delights in deflating what he has an American Indian call the "rank presumption" of trying to convince people that "a man had died on a tree to save them all" (26). For Gaddis, the fate of Christianity "hung on a diphthong" (9), the author's satiric comment on the Council of Nicea's debate as to whether *homoousian* (same) or *homoiousian* (like) was the correct scriptural interpretation of the substance of God / Jesus (9).

An even stronger critique of past mythic systems is mirrored by the fate of the characters in the novel who most intertwine with Wyatt's life. All manifest references to past ideals, but all are miserable failures in their own quests for redemption. Valentine, the Gnostic art critic who aspires to protect the beautiful from the vulgar masses, dies an insomniac. Wyatt's father, the erudite Reverend Gwyon, realizes the synchronic nature of religion yet is doomed to the madness of preaching Mithraism to a timid group of Protestant women. Esme, Wyatt's heroin-addicted model / lover, dies from kissing the diseased foot of a statue of Saint Peter, and Stanley, the devout Catholic whose sole purpose for living is to dedicate an organ mass to his dead mother, is buried alive when the first notes of the mass he plays cause the collapse of the church at the novel's end. Anselm, named after the saint who introduced an important doctrine of atonement to Christianity, is a nihilist who eventually castrates himself and sells his memoirs, an event sardonically described as "the biggest thing since the _Confessions_" (935).

In contrast to the perceived failures of conventional mythic systems to acknowledge, preserve, and transform humanity, the power of Wyatt's alchemical art appears promising. At first glance, such a claim seems incapable of being substantiated, because in _The Recognitions_ art, including Wyatt's, is inextricably bound up with forgery and counterfeit. As Wyatt explains to Valentine, however, there are qualitatively different types of forgeries. Whereas some people might seek fame and fortune by passing off their counterfeits as originals, Wyatt's copying is motivated by something else: "Do you think I do these the way all other forging has been done? No, it's . . . the recognitions go much deeper, much further back. . . . The experts with their photomicrography and macrophotography, do you think that's all there is to it? Some of them aren't fools, they don't just look for a hat or a beard, or a style they can recognize, they look with memories that . . . go beyond themselves, that go back to . . . where mine goes" (250). Wyatt's memory goes back to the fifteenth century, when the dedication and goals of the guild artist were in effect alchemical in nature: "I'm a master painter in the Guild, in Flanders. . . . I've taken the Guild oath, not for the critics, the experts. . . . You, you have no more to do with me than if you are my descendants, nothing to do with me. The Guild oath, to use pure materials, to work in the sight of God" (250). Wyatt's justification for his forgery, in other words, is a proper attitude toward his work, a desire to reach the genuine through a kind of mystical participation with the artists whose works he forged. Dedicated art, Gaddis seems to say, can transform, can through its redemptive power serve as an alchemical process of secular salvation. In a brilliant stroke, Gaddis affirms this idea by having Wyatt mention Fermat's last theorem, a mathematical postulate tantalizingly unproven at the time Gaddis wrote the novel.[15] The significance of this reference to alchemical art (no one but Wyatt understands the reference) is that although the theorem had not yet been proven, it was conceivable that it could be. That is, unlike the hocus-pocus of transmuting lead into gold or squaring the circle, conundrums normally associated with exoteric alchemy, Wyatt's alchemical quest to find his version of the *prima materia* seems plausible. Wyatt is the adept in this novel, and his devotion to alchemy rather than to science or religion makes him the most significant character in *The Recognitions*, for it is Wyatt who rejects the role of priest for that of artist / alchemist.[16]

Having inextricably bound alchemy to art as the preferred means for salvation, however, Gaddis goes on to undercut the possibility of artistic transformation by focusing on artistic imitation, an activity that can and does leave room for charges of forgery and fraud.

Early in the novel, Wyatt finances his escape from Aunt May by scrupulously copying a Bosch table depicting the seven deadly sins and then selling it to an elderly art collector, the Count de Brescia (59). This character is a clear allusion to Adano de Brescia, a counterfeiter who resides in the tenth bolgia of the eighth circle of hell in Dante's *Inferno*, where people suffer who have committed four types of fraud: alchemy, false witness, counterfeiting, and evil impersonation. What Gaddis brings to mind through this reference becomes a central focus of the novel: Does the genius exist in the midst of the fraud and duplicity that floods the book, and if so, is alchemical art the correct way of reaching it?

As stated earlier, the novel is replete with counterfeiters— Sinisterra, Valentine, Otto, Recktall Brown—all characters from whom Wyatt dissociates himself. In openly acknowledging his

copying and lack of originality, Wyatt at first seems free from
perpetrating fraud. Yet Wyatt, too, is finally guilty of fraud, and
of the most insidious kind: the unconscious fraud of assuming
that there was an original at all. The possibility that no genuine,
no *prima materia* exists, is brought up several times in the novel.
As Wyatt puts it in describing the act of copying the Bosch table,
"Copying a copy? Is that where I started? . . . Now if there was
no gold? . . . And if what I've been forging does not exist?"
(381). Later, upon discovering that the Bosch he copied was, in
fact, an original, Wyatt exclaims, "Yes, thank God there was
gold to forge!" (689). Wyatt mistakenly assumes the existence
of an original, some alchemical stone with which one can establish
connection with the universe. Wyatt fails to recognize, however,
that the quest for purity and authenticity may itself be motivated
by the neurotic fear that such purity and authenticity do not
exist. Valentine, whose name not only alludes to a fraudulent
alchemist but also to a Gnostic high priest, reminds Wyatt of
this in the following passage:

> Vulgarity, cupidity and power, is that what frightens you? Is that all
> you see around you and you think it was all like the adoration of
> the mystic lamb. . . . Yes, I remember your little talk, your insane
> upside-down apology for these pictures, every figure and object with
> its own presence, its own consciousness because it was being looked
> at by God! Do you know what it was? What it really was? That
> everything was so afraid, so uncertain God saw it, that it insisted its
> vanities on His eyes. . . . Because maybe God isn't watching. Maybe
> he doesn't see. . . . Separation . . . all of it cluttered with separation
> everything in its own vain shell, everything separate, withdrawn
> from everything else Being looked at by God! Is there separation in
> God? (689–90)

Like the Flemish painters Valentine describes, Wyatt is motivated by fear, a fear that extends to shunning of his wife, his

friends, and humanity in general because contact with them might sully his craft. Earlier in the novel, Wyatt defines the basis of his aesthetic, a quality he observes in a performance of flamenco music as the "precision of suffering": "That's what it is, this arrogance, in this flamenco music this same arrogance of suffering, listen. The strength of it's what's so overpowering, the self-sufficiency that's so delicate and tender without an instant of sentimentality. With infinite pity but refusing pity, it's a precision of suffering—the tremendous tension of violence all enclosed in a framework . . . in a pattern that doesn't pretend to any other level but its own" (111). It is significant that flamenco means "Flemish" in Spanish, a meaning that conflates Wyatt's concern with alchemical precision with Valentine's critique of the Flemish painters to reinforce the idea that although suffering is necessary for redemption, it is insufficient insofar as it focuses on privacy and doubt. Wyatt's wife, Esther, reminds the reader of this when she tells Wyatt, "Precision of suffering . . . privacy of suffering . . . if that's what it is, suffering, then you . . . share it" (116). In shunning vulgarity, using only pure materials, and accepting the necessity of suffering, Wyatt attempts to transform his world without participating in it.

Yet as Valentine reminds the reader, in life as in alchemy, the matter to be redeemed, the *prima materia,* is most impure and vulgar, requiring an active engagement on the part of anyone desiring to transform it. Valentine states that Recktall Brown, the member of the art scheme that Wyatt shuns, "does not understand reality. . . . Recktall Brown is Reality . . . a very different thing" (244). Brown, in his most Freudian aspect, is the character that Wyatt should engage but never does, for only by plunging oneself into a world of detritus that Wyatt studiously avoids can one truly begin the transformational process. Wyatt's life is riddled by guilt, the source of which Gaddis explains through situations amenable to both Freudian and Jungian theory. Haunted by the memory of his mother and dominated by the bizarre eccentricities of his father, Wyatt's "truth" becomes those unresolved issues of origin toward which Wyatt generates behavior as a response. Only when Wyatt acts on the truth of Jung's statement that "all neurosis is a substitute for legitimate suffering" can he begin to understand reality. Wyatt was right in focusing on the significance of the suffering, but his refusal to deal with the personal suffering connected with his mother and father kept his suffering both private and so neurotic. Only when he begins to share his suffering, to extend his reach past himself to others, does his martyrdom become significant, transforming him from the "lonely little boy getting upset over silly people" (118) that Wyatt steadfastly remained through most of the novel into Stephen, not only the first Christian martyr but also the name his mother, Camilla, originally intended for him (27).

This is the idea of transformation that informs the idea of alchemy as the novel ends. Wyatt / Stephen realizes that the constancy of the *lapis*, the philosopher's stone of purity he sought in his quest for the genuine in art, is really constant change and that the only transformation possible is self-transformation. Gaddis dramatizes this recognition by having Stephen, already having dropped a portrait of his father to the ground, make the gesture of passing his mother's earrings to the daughter he has fathered with the prostitute, Pastora, freeing himself to follow the dictum he announces at this point in the novel: "Dilige et quod vis fac" (899). Informed by a sense of agapistic love and engaged in the activity of scraping paintings down to the bare canvas, Stephen has come to realize that art, like science and religion, is a fraudulent myth. The only material to be transformed is the self, something Stephen acknowledges when he says "Now at last, to live deliberately" (900). Like Thoreau, Stephen has set aside preconceived notions of truth in favor of discovering what the nature of the Melvillian white pasteboard canvas of reality might contain.

Even so, lest the reader attach too much significance to this event, Gaddis undercuts any collective significance to Stephen's singular transformation in the remaining fifty-six pages of the novel. Offsetting Stephen's Thoreauvean pronouncements is a complex mix of calamities punctuated by the church's collapse in the last lines of the novel, reminding readers in turn of the collapse of any singular solution. In this sense, Gaddis's method of juxtaposing these myths in *The Recognitions* reminds one of Joyce's attitude toward essential being lampooned in the portmanteau term "contrajewbangconsubstantiality": no matter how much humanity may seek a single essence, the experience of the quest teaches that Arius was right in the realization that the illusion of essence is all there is. As Steven Moore adeptly points out, in *The Recognitions* Wyatt / Stephen comes to the same recognition that the alchemist Michal Majer discovered: the *lapis*, the unchanging essence is at best confined to fiction: "At the end of his chef-d'oeuvre he confesses that in the course of his grand *peregrinatio* he found neither Mercurus [the philosophical stone] nor the phoenix [of immortality], but only a feather—his pen! This is a delicate hint at his realization that the great adventure had led to nothing beyond his copious literary achievement."[17] The only "essence" to which myth refers—artistic or religious, alchemical as well as scientific—is linguistic, a mix of copious literary achievements whose mutually exclusive claims are catalogued by *The Recognitions*.

Read in this manner, as a novel that dramatizes what Alfred North Whitehead called "the burden of inert ideas," *The Recognitions* confirms what Jack Goody and Ian Wyatt point out in "The Consequences of Literacy": Literate society accumulates such a vast repertoire of knowledge about itself without the palliative of cultural amnesia available to primitive cultures that "the content of the cultural tradition grows continuously, and insofar as it affects any particular individual he becomes a palimpsest composed of layers of beliefs and attitudes belonging to different stages of historical time."[18]

It is certainly this burden of the dross of the past that haunts Wyatt. A literate man seeking redemption in a world informed by a farrago of systems, Wyatt is literally confused throughout much of the novel as thoughts of Arius or Aristotle surface and confuse discussions of housekeeping or upcoming events (57–62). Gaddis's point seems clear: to seek redemption in a world informed by such contradiction leads to a reification of consciousness that becomes unbearable. As Wyatt puts it, "Why, all this around us is for people who can keep their balance only in the light, where they move as though nothing were fragile, nothing tempered by possibility, and all of a sudden—bang! Something breaks. Then you have to stop and put the pieces together again . . . until you've broken it and picked up the pieces enough times, and you have the whole thing in its all its dimensions. But the discipline the detail . . . sometimes the accumulation is too much to bear" (113–14).

As both Goody and Wyatt suggest and as Wyatt's actions confirm, to live in such a way actually becomes a form of societal death:

From the standpoint of the individual intellectual, of the literate specialist, the vista of endless choices and discoveries offered by so extensive a past can be a source of great stimulation and interest, but when we consider the social effects of such orientation, it becomes apparent that this situation fosters the alienation that has characterized so many writers and philosophers of the West since the twentieth century. It was surely, for example, this lack of social amnesia in alphabetic cultures that led Nietzsche to describe "we moderns" as "wandering encyclopedias unable to live and act in the present and obsessed by a historical sense that injures and finally destroys the living thing, be it a man or a system or a culture."[19]

In the climate of overwhelming detail that pervades the novel, the proliferation of systems is so presented that no unifying thesis can be drawn from them; or rather, the allusions to so many different ways of structuring are meant to suggest the inevitable futility of such a quest. As Wyatt, in response to his wife Esther's claim that he has "abdicated life," explains: "But the past—every instance the past is reshaping itself, it shifts and breaks and changes, and every minute we were finding, I was right, I was wrong, until . . . " (590).

The preceding lines summarize the effect of the vision of alterity offered up in the novel: the frustration its characters experience at trying to recover some singular meaning within a fragmented landscape. Alchemy, following Jung's interpretation, is Gaddis's reminder that the work of redemption—each person's quest for "integration of his personality"—is the responsibility of those who seek it. Yet so long as one assumes that the goal is absolute, that there is "gold to forge," and that the singular genius of the *archeus* is the means of achieving it, the redemptive quest will remain inadequate in a world that intractably resists singular solutions.

Gaddis not only demonstrates the counterfeit nature of essential structure within the novel; he also makes the act of reading *The Recognitions* correlative with the dilemma faced by the characters. Gaddis extends the same sense of frustration to the reader by disappointing expectations of narrative form that the reader traditionally brings to a text. This strategy manifests itself in several ways. Within the catalog of myths, for example, the reader finds allusions to two systems with qualitatively different premises than those of Christianity, science, or alchemical art. If the characters are denied a solution, perhaps readers can still enact "the mythical method," engage their critical *archeus* to recover a sufficient number of fragments to create a coherent interpretation.

One such system, the source of Wyatt's family name, is Robert Graves's seminal account of the "waxing and waning power" of the matriarchal muse—*The White Goddess*.[20] First published while Gaddis was composing *The Recognitions*, *The White Goddess* shares the former's concern with counterfeit and the deformation of tradition. According to Graves, there was a time "Before Religion" (Gaddis's expression, p. 12) in which the celebration of ritual was in essence one of atonement via the poetic process, an act of propitiation toward a matriarchal goddess that man worshipped selflessly as his creator, teacher, and destroyer. After establishing his thesis, Graves argues that the historical rise of such patriarchal systems as Christianity upset the rhythmic balance inherent in matriarchal worship, turning what Graves refers to as syncretic ritual into separate religions with each sect positing the god of their most powerful enemy as the devil. As Graves describes it, "As soon as Apollo the organizer, God of science, usurps the power of his mother, Goddess of inspired truth, wisdom, and poetry, who tries to bind her devotees by laws—inspired magic goes, and what remains is theology, ecclesiastical ritual and negatively ethical behavior,"[21] lines Gaddis recasts in *The Recognitions* when he writes "There was, in fact, a religious aura about this festival, religious that is in the sense of devotion, adoration, celebration of deity, before religion became confused with systems of ethics and morality to become a sore affliction upon the very things it had once exalted" (311).

To such "sore affliction" visited upon the matriarchal tradition, Graves offers the following alternative: that the poet, who in ur-

form is Gwyion, will revive the ancient poetic traditions that
the organized church has reviled by returning to the one story
that has meaning: celebration of the goddess of the moon.

Another mythic system of lunar origin alluded to in *The Recognitions* is gnosticism. As Hans Jonas points out in *The Gnostic
Religion*, the *Clementine Recognitions* consists of Peter's disputations with the Gnostic Simon Magus, reputed by Christians to
be "the father of all heresy" although in fact offering a rival
message of prior and independent origin to Christianity.[22] As did
worshippers of the White Goddess, Gnostics located salvation in
the waxing and waning power of the moon, the domain of Pistis
Sophia. As Rose Arthur points out in *The Wisdom Goddess*,
analysis of Nag Hammadi manuscripts implies that Gnostic doctrine exhibited a pervasive feminine character. If Christianity
emphasized knowledge of God through his masculine mediator,
Jesus Christ, "the secret gnosis in non-Christian texts often pertains to a feminine deity, called Sophia, who links created and
non-created being. The gnostic condition depends upon a pneumatic relationship with her who is at once the content of knowledge and the agent by which her worshippers attain gnosis."[23]
As a personification of wisdom, Sophia both reveals truth and
dramatizes it through her fall and redemption. This truth is gnosis,
or self-knowledge, characterized by Jonas as *via negationis*, a
"learned ignorance" of limits, detachment, and humility.

With the knowledge of these concepts, a reader could consider
the idea that amid the landscape of failed patriarchal myths, order
can be recovered. The insight might be denied to the characters
of *The Recognitions*, but for the reader the message seems to be
to revert to the matriarchal system. Replace the masculine drives
for power and control with humility and sacrifice, and the unifying
power of the matriarchal myth can reassemble this fragmented
culture.

The problem with such a reading is that it distorts and reduces the novel. In contrast to the idyllic golden age described by Graves, the temporal setting of *The Recognitions* is decidedly a time after matriarchal magic "had despaired and become religion" (12), a time after the overwhelming defeat of gnosticism by patriarchal Christianity. In the intervening millennia since these events, the power of patriarchal religion, however wrongheaded, grew exponentially. With the comprehensive survey of historical culture that the novel offers, it would be naive to argue for a return to matriarchy. The novel reinforces this by having every feminine goddess character in the novel either corrupted or destroyed by society, and Valentine's death—he dies a babbling insomniac—speaks to the limits of the Gnostic alternative. In any case, these are also mythic systems, claiming exclusive knowledge of the truth and of the means for one to reach it. To be sure, there is a vertical component to Gaddis's thematology—i.e., Gnostic is better than Christian because the former is more inclusive—but finally the strategy is to reveal the inevitable falsification of all mythic structures. In the idiom of alchemy, Gaddis uses myths to satirize the hermetic truth "as above / so below" by showing that all mythic systems, patriarchal and matriarchal, are identical in the negative sense that they offer a nostalgia for the type of unified explanation of reality that is no longer acceptable.

Denied resolution by the content of the book, readers of *The Recognitions* turn their attention to the style of the novel to find ways of recovering a unified reading of the text. Once more, however, readers have their expectations disappointed, because the narrative form also subverts unified interpretation.

Steven Moore, for example, traces the way that hours and days are repeated, mixed up, or omitted in the novel, distorting the sense of temporal form normally made manifest in the reader's sequential experience of a work.[24] In turn, this chronological confusion points to an even more fundamental structural ambiguity in *The Recognitions*, the nature of its plot.

The Recognitions does not have a conventional plot—or more accurately, everything in the novel is plot. Flashbacks, bits of dialogue from other times and places, sudden shifts of scene and personae are all placed at an equal distance from the reader. By not distinguishing between meaningful and irrelevant background detail, as most traditional novels do, *The Recognitions* establishes a link between the reader's experience of the text and the central theme of discontinuity presented within it. Because the novel always undercuts the significance of any particular event, the readers' expectations of conventional aesthetic closure are never fulfilled. As a result, their attempts to structure the action of the novel are as futile as the attempts of the characters inside the novel to order their world.

Among the numerous examples in *The Recognitions*, the incident of the cross-eyed girl stands out as one that dramatizes the futility of any attempt by the reader to transmute aesthetically significant meaning from the dross of the novel.

The first reference to the cross-eyed girl occurs right after Gwyon has buried Wyatt's mother. Returning home from her first communion, the girl was raped and killed by a man infected with a disease that he believed could be cured if he had intercourse with a virgin (16). The local pharmacist of San Zwingli tells Gwyon that the little girl would make a perfect patron for the town, but the cost of canonization would be prohibitive (17). At this point the subject appears closed, but references to it reappear at several different points in the novel that bear no apparent relation to its original context.

On page 291, for example, a newspaper account stressing the horrific aspects of the girl's death appears while the reader is struggling to understand why "that colossus of self-justification, 'Reason' " is described as a "triumphal abortion" (290). Later, after Agnes Deigh has jumped from the window of her apartment only to survive by landing on a mailman, the reader suddenly discovers that the little girl's attacker was misidentified and that the misidentified person is suing the paper for four million lire (740). The final mention of the cross-eyed girl occurs at the end of the novel. After stabbing Valentine and believing himself to be a fugitive, Wyatt flees to San Zwingli to search for Camilla's grave. There he meets up with Sinisterra, the man responsible for Camilla's death and the one who provides Wyatt with a new identity, a forged Swiss passport of Stephen Asche. Sinisterra, who has renamed himself Mr. Yák to avoid detection, involves Wyatt / Stephen in a scheme to exhume a corpse and sell it as an Egyptian mummy. At this point, Yák tells Stephen about the canonization of the cross-eyed girl, who is buried next to Camilla, including the peculiar fact that when "they took her out of the graveyard here to put her somewhere else when she was beatified, they thought she looked kind of big for an eleven year-old girl" (791). Stephen realizes that Camilla has been exhumed and can-onized instead of the cross-eyed girl, a recognition graphically described by the priest who breaks open the casket: "Cuno! . . . Dios! Valgome Dios!" (Fuck! God! So help me God!) (792).

Conventional wisdom on the novel suggests that at this junc-ture the random events appear to take on some larger meaning.[25] The cross-eyed girl provides an efficient scaffolding for Wyatt's redemption, albeit in burlesque fashion. Up to this point in the novel Wyatt has suffered from the guilt of not accepting his mother's death, a guilt symbolized by his unfinished painting of Camilla known as the *Stabat Mater*. With his recognition of her sainthood, Wyatt is now freed to become the person his mother intended, Stephen Gwyon, because Stephen was the name Camilla originally chose for him before Aunt May "peremptorily supplied the name Wyatt from somewhere in the Gwyon genealogy" (271).

A closer reading shows, however, that Gaddis deftly undercuts the possibility that the presence of the cross-eyed girl can be understood as some leitmotiv with which the reader may assemble some semblance of significant narrative closure. The name on the passport forged by Mr. Yák is Stephen Asche. The last name foreshadows Gaddis's final comment on the possibility of reaching closure, for the reader as well as the characters. Reverend Gwyon is cremated; his ashes are mistaken for wheat germ and sent abroad, finally winding up in Spain, where they are baked into bread that Stephen eats. The underlying grim humor of this sequence, then, amounts to a parody of reaching consubstantiality. Through it, Gaddis once more reminds the reader that all ceremony is conceit and that the facts of the novel will always exceed the reader's ability to grasp them completely and consistently. As the cross-eyed girl motif indicates, readers first fail to recognize the significance of the apparently trivial and unrelated references. Once they manage to fit the pieces of the narrative puzzle together, the significance of the effort is undercut by the tone of the result. By trying to join with the narrative, in other words, the reader's union with the text mirrors Stephen's parodistic state of consubstantiality with the good reverend. Both quests, for reader as well as character, demonstrate that no higher, meaningful union is possible.

Even the sentence style of *The Recognitions* suggests the theme of essential indeterminacy for the reader. As John Leverence's insightful study shows, the prominent mark of punctuation in the novel is the ellipsis, creating an unfinished style that Morris W. Croll describes as the "loose" style of Baroque prose.[26] Croll writes, "The loose baroque sentence begins without premedation, stating its idea in the first form that occurs; the second member (clause) is determined by the situation in which the mind finds itself after the first has been spoken; and so on throughout the period (sentence), each member being an emerging of the situation (since each is suddenly called for by what preceded it). The period, in theory at least, is not made: it becomes. It completes itself and takes on a form in the course of the motion of mind which it expresses."[27]

The significance of writing sentences this way, a style present on every page of *The Recognitions*, is that it undercuts and even mocks the more formal conventions found in the more common serial or curt style. As Croll describes it, this curt style, used to support "timeless aphorisms and other meditations," depends for its full effect on a union of formal traits "as rigorous and unalterable as if they were prescribed by rule."[28] In contrast, the loose baroque style mimicked by Gaddis gives writing the effect of being, not the result of a meditation, but the actual meditation in progress, "a process where the reader watches the pen move and stop as the writer thinks."[29] The style does not encourage abstract reflective thinking about its content; instead, it helps maintain the verisimilitude of unstructured content in the process of being created.

In form as well as content, for the reader as well as the characters, *The Recognitions* gives no warrant for belief in recovering meaning by means of an essential structure. In concept, the collage of the novel presents a linguistic version of the same complementary universe faced by quantum physics. The reader is forced to accept the second order, meta-ethical tenet of the ethics of indeterminacy: the description of the alterity of reality that intractably resists formulations that claim to be more exact than probability allows.

But to use language simply to demonstrate the fraudulence of essential structure by itself does not justify how humane values have a place in a world of essential indeterminacy and does not answer the question of how Gaddis puts forth a vision of an agapistic love informed by a sense of alterity and transformation in this book. Instead, we must consider how this novel creates conditions that allow the reader to collaborate in creating the text's meaning by highlighting the virtues of risk-taking and responsible suffering that together make up the first-order virtues of Gaddis's agapistic ethic. In examining these conditions, *The Recognitions* can be understood to suggest a way to live deliberately in a world without absolutes, for it teaches the reader how to recover meaning from an indeterminate text and, by extension, how to recover meaning within an indeterminate world.

The means of enacting the first-order ethics is allusion, but it is a type different from the mythic allusions already discussed. Along with those references that help to illuminate the counterfeit nature of religious, scientific, and artistic mythic quests for unconditioned order, the novel also presents a smattering of allusions to the poet Rainer Maria Rilke that are seemingly extraneous, clarifying neither the quest for redemption nor the impossibility of achieving it. Because these allusions do not seem to fit the concerns of the text, the reader might reasonably question their purpose. One possible answer is, of course, that Gaddis simply put everything he knew into the book.[30] Another answer is to see allusions to Rilke as part of Gaddis's careful rhetorical plan to teach readers how to read *The Recognitions*.

A cursory reading of the allusions to Rilke in *The Recognitions* suggests that their presence merely lends further support to the venality present in the novel. At Esther's Christmas Eve party, for example, the poet Max is exposed for plagiarizing the first *Duino Elegy* (622). The first line of this elegy, "Who, if I cried / Would hear me among the angelic orders?" appears at several points throughout the novel, apparently reflecting the greedy and solipsistic condition in which most of the characters find themselves. Another possible interpretation of Rilke's presence in the novel is that the allusions are parodistic, a means for

Gaddis to underscore further the discrepancy between the ideal
claims of art and the actual uses to which it is put. One could
argue, for example, that Gaddis is parodying the last lines of the
Duino Elegies when he describes on the novel's last page the
collapse of the church at Fenestrula: "Everything moved, and
even in falling, soared in atonement" (956). Considered more
carefully, however, the allusions to Rilke are much more than
simple parodies. The allusions to Rilke should be considered as
parabolic, heuristic rhetorical devices that redirect the reader
away from concern with redemption to a consideration of the
nature of meaning itself, helping readers to learn a new understanding of meaning—and value—so that they can understand
the novel in new ways. This analysis does not mean to suggest
that the allusions to Rilke in *The Recognitions* provide the key to
the meaning of the novel, for that would mean absolutizing Rilke.
Rather the allusions to Rilke—and there may be others I have
failed to recognize—invite the reader to engage in constructive
interpretation, to embrace the challenge of a textual world without absolutes by wresting these thought fragments out of their
original context to read what was never written.

As scholarship on the subject suggests, parable usually takes
the form of a narrative riddle whose subject remains hidden so
long as interpretation is confined within the action of the narrative.[31] The meaning of the parable becomes clear only when
readers learn to stand outside the narrative and to realize that
the solution appears not in the form of an answer but as a calling
into question of the interpretative assumptions they bring to the
text. The true subject of most parables is the nature of interpretative understanding itself; parables are narratives about the reader's
experience of reading parables.

Considering the allusions to Rilke in this manner, it is possible
to argue that their purpose is not to provide a set of answers to
the question posed by the text's characters concerning how to

achieve a conventional sort of redemption but instead to help the readers themselves formulate new questions about what constitutes redemption, questions that lead them in another direction altogether. As readers investigate allusions to Rilke in this way, they discover that the poet was not concerned with achieving conventional redemption at all. Instead, Rilke felt that humanity's true purpose was to turn away from such transcendent quests to recover what the poet called an Orphic sensibility: the belief that life and death are interdependent states linked through the power of love.

The critical strategy on which this interpretation depends is the disorientation that readers experience when they explore the allusions to Rilke in detail. Expecting to find ideas that reinforce the novel's concern with essential structure and the problems involved in achieving it, readers instead discover a totally different premise: the concern with essential transformation.

The elegies were a turning point in Rilke's career; he previously had struggled "from outward form to win / the passion and the life, whose fountains are within."[32] In the elegies, however, Rilke turned away from what he called a "romantic" concern with external forms, instead wanting to fashion, as J. B. Leishman puts it, "some ultimate vision of human life and destiny and of the true relationship between the looker and that world on which he had looked so intensely."[33] In the process of defining and facing the terms of human existence, the elegies focus on death and its attendant sufferings: loss, pain, illness, irreparable distress. But this concern with death is not morbid; instead, it is meant as a corrective for humanity's tendency to avoid death, a tendency that Rilke felt caused people to avoid life. As Rilke elaborated to his Polish translator, "Affirmation of life and death appear as one in the *Elegies*. To admit the one without the other is, as is here learned and celebrated, a limitation that in the end excludes all infinity. Death is *the side of life* that is turned away from us.

We must try to achieve the fullest conclusion of our existence, which is at home in the two unseparated realms, inexhaustibly nourished by both"[34] The vision of existence that informs the elegies is not dualistic, life versus death, but complementary:

> It is not a question of pleasing
> nor of conversion
> provided that we know to
> obey complementary orders.[35]

Although Rilke's insights about the interpenetration of life and death do not account for everything the *Duino Elegies* tell us, they mark the distinctive territory of the poems and lead one to explore the role of man in this climate. In the elegies, the condition of life is transitory, contradicting the illusory ideal of some permanently satisfying state. Yet humans' limitation paradoxically is seen by Rilke as the necessary precondition for their special power and purpose, without which they could not hope to experience reality. Instead of seeking to transcend death, which is impossible, humanity should seek to transform the otherwise transitory state of visible existence into "invisible vibrations." As Rilke explains,

> Nature, the things we move among and use, are provisional and perishable; but, so long as we are here, they are our possessions. . . . Hence it is important not only to run down and degrade everything earthly, but just because of its temporariness, which it shares with us, we ought to grasp and transform these phenomena and these things in a most loving understanding. Transform: Yes; for our task is so deeply and so passionately to impress upon ourselves this provisional and perishable earth that its essential being will arise "invisibly" within us. . . . The *Elegies* show us at this work, this work of continual transformation of the dear visible and tangible into the invisible

vibrations and agitations of our own nature, which introduces vibration numbers into the vibration spheres of the universe.[36]

Rilke attests to this notion of transformation in the ninth elegy
when he writes:

Earth, isn't this what you want; an invisible
re-arising within us? Is it not your dream
to be one day invisible? Earth! Invisible!
What is your urgent command, if
not transformation?[37]

The cost of achieving transformation is high. Unlike the mysterious angel present in the *Duino Elegies*, humans can experience
true transformation only at the cost of their identity, their claim
of ownership over life. As Geoffrey Hartman describes it, in
Rilke's aesthetic "the will to possession is discounted for the will
to experience without hope for possession."[38] The sacrifice of
individuality in turn points to another difficult aspect of Rilke's
aesthetic: the unqualified acceptance of the condition of suffering.
To understand transformation, one must first accept the essential
pain of life as portrayed in the elegies. In spite of the toll death
takes, in spite of the inevitable breakdown between lovers, humans should neither abandon nor resist their painful fate. Instead
they become visionaries who see, through the act of suffering,
to the essence of the thing that suffers, a recognition necessary
before transformation can occur.

Although it is true, as an unnamed critic in *The Recognitions*
states, "that Rilke's references were occasionally *obscure*" (577),
their disclosure provides the reader with important new insights.
If the reader takes the critic's hint and considers the obscure
allusions to the poet in the parabolic way described above, Rilke
becomes more than a means of underscoring or parodying suffering

in the novel; he provides the means of transforming this suffering. As the same unnamed critic explains, "I understand Rilke, I understand because he respected human suffering, not like those snotty kids who are writing now" (577). Armed with the outlook that suffering is something to be respected rather than shunned, the reader can return to the novel to reconsider the problems of essential structure and redemption in ways not permitted by information and events contained within the text. This reconstruction manifests itself in two ways: thematically and structurally.

Thematically, the reference to Gwyon's mountain, Mt. Lamentation (50), can now be understood as more than simply a passing reference to regret. Lamentation is also the setting for the tenth elegy, the work that concludes Rilke's theme that humanity's goal is neither an appeasement in life nor a happiness in death but an understanding of the complementaries, life and death.

Understanding Rilke in the ways described above also allows the reader to reinterpret the structural use of the ellipsis within the novel. Rilke made use of the ellipsis in the _Duino Elegies_, but not to indicate the sense of unstructured process, as Croll suggests. Instead, Rilke used the ellipsis to indicate what he called "the end of the sayable," that point where the limit of conceptualization is reached and the experience of transformation begins.[39] Like the reader of the elegies, the reader of _The Recognitions_ is asked to go past the perceived limits of conceptual understanding to transform the novel through the experiential activity of bringing new information to it.

Following this idea, the most important information the reader can transform surrounds the novel's protagonist. As previously noted, within textual limits Wyatt / Stephen is a failed alchemist. Unable to redeem himself through his art, by the novel's end he is reduced to scraping old paintings down to their original canvas,

Gaddis's comment on the necessity of deconstructing art that attempts to fraudulently structure the white pasteboard of reality. Armed with the new insights that they bring to the text, however, readers can in effect transform Wyatt's condition at the end of the novel to one of affirmation. Throughout *The Recognitions* Wyatt has been haunted by "the intimacies of catoptric communion," the specter of his own image that constantly appears in the mirrors he uses to create forgeries of masterpieces (673). At the novel's end, however, Wyatt / Stephen can be understood to dramatize the truth annunciated by Rilke: that one can transform narcissistic mirrors into what the poet called "objective" and "impersonal" ones. By representing heretofore oppressive experiences fully yet denying them any personal significance, Rilke looked into such mirrors and said, "not this refers to me, but—this is" (nicht: das bin ich; nein dies ist).[40]

In living with the Spanish prostitute Pastora, in fathering a child "not born, but borne out of love" (897–98), in scraping counterfeit paintings down to their genuine white pasteboard, Stephen dramatizes what it means to look into the impersonal mirror to which Rilke refers. As his name change, Camilla's mistaken sainthood, and the parody of reaching consubstantiality with Gwyon all make clear, the significance of existence is not in answering the narcissistic question, "Am I the man for whom Christ died?" (440). Like Rilke, Stephen has come to admire El Greco, and in losing what Rilke called *platz angst* (the fear of spaces that Valentine claimed was the reason for the myriad of detail in fifteenth-century Flemish paintings), Stephen comes to the recognition that, like El Greco, "we all study with Titian: yes he studied with Titian. That's where El Greco learned, that's where he learned to simplify . . . that's where he learned not to be afraid of spaces, not to get lost in details and clutter, and separate everything" (872).[41] Changing his credo from *Cave, Cave, Dominus Videt* (Beware, Beware, God sees) to Augustine's

Dilige et quod vis fac (Love and do what you will) by the end of the novel, Stephen has come to recognize the essential truth of Rilke's vision: In a world that lacks sacred truth, humanity's purpose is the transformation of Jung's concept of legitimate suffering. As Stephen explains to the novelist Ludy, "I told you, there was a moment in travel when love and necessity became the same thing. And now, if the Gods themselves cannot recall their gifts, we must live them through, and redeem them" (898).

This attitude closely parallels Rilke's solution to the problem of why we exist. For Rilke, the purpose of our existence is not knowledge or experience; we exist because existence is in itself of value and because everything that exists depends on the transformational act of making everyone an inward and invisible part of ourselves. "We have received from earth," Rilke says, "so deeply and so passionately a mandate to impress upon ourselves this provisional and perishable earth, that its essential being will arise again 'invisibly' within us."[42]

After once more echoing Thoreau's ideal of "Yes. We'll simplify, Hear?" (900), Stephen vanishes, a disappearance that has both thematic and structural significance.

Thematically, he vanishes because he has found an alternative to the self-consuming doubt that has haunted him throughout the novel, an alternative dramatized by his departure to find his and Pastora's daughter. Structurally, Stephen vanishes because he is no longer needed as a teacher. The reader has "used him up" by learning his lesson—the lesson of how to read the novel. The knowledge of Rilke enables readers to understand how they as well as Stephen might avoid the fate of a failed alchemist who vainly seeks pure, unsullied materials as the basis for transformation and redemption. By reading Rilke and then bringing this knowledge to Gaddis's novel, the reader has also learned how to read *The Recognitions* in a new way that permits a positive understanding of a book whose conventional wisdom is bleak, sardonic, and despairing. This new way of reading emphasizes the reader's role as a collaborator who goes outside the novel to bring back new information with which to transform fictive landscapes of lamentation into ones where meaning and significance of a certain sort exist. Read in this manner, the novel is no longer perceived as a completed text retrospectively interpreted by a passive reader. Instead, *The Recognitions* becomes what Rilke called in the tenth elegy an "indescribable outline / as if on the doubly opened / pages of a Book," a provisional text, already lying open, whose structure is complete (in the sense of being understood) only when the reader paradoxically opens it again by actively collaborating in its construction.[43] Gaddis's use of the oblique allusions to Rilke dramatize the virtue of the first-order ethics of indeterminacy, attesting to the tenets of risk-taking and suffering by requiring that the reader actively engage the novel to recover meaning from it.

In using this type of allusion to illustrate in significant ways a premise that the text itself does not consider in any traditional sense, Gaddis changes the ritual of reading the novel. The textual event of unconventional allusions disappoints his narrative expectations. These unfulfilled expectations, however, are not ends in themselves, but rather, they represent means by which the author can lead the reader to a new awareness of understanding. The disappointment of expectation pushes readers to formulate solutions of their own and, in so doing, come to realize their role as collaborator as well as reader. In this sense the source of the novel's title is as much Rilke's *Sonnets to Orpheus* as it is the *Clementine Recognitions*. As sonnet twelve of book two reminds us: "The Recognition recognizes him who pours himself forth as a spring" ("Wer Sichh als quelle ergiesst / den erkennt die Erkennung").[44] In Rilke's Orphic vision, life has meaning only when one "pours himself" into life, when one recognizes that all transformation is self-transformation, including the transformation of the role of the reader. Gaddis's unconventional use of allusion clarifies the inescapable role collaboration plays in the construction of meaning, enforcing this principle by making the reader recapitulate its premise through the experience of reading *The Recognitions*.

But if Gaddis helps readers grasp what it means to live it through in a world where discriminating between the genuine power of transformation and its counterfeit has become difficult, he also anticipates the world of *J R*, where everything has become counterfeit, where the doctrine of simplification is reduced to the catch phrase for an advertising executive, where value has been transfigured into commodity, where the sense of the genuine, as Wyatt describes it, is "irretrievably lost": "there is always the sense . . . the sense of recalling something, of almost reaching it, and holding it . . . and then it's . . . escaped again. It's escaped again, and there's only a sense of disappointment, of something irretrievably lost" (119). In *The Recognitions* Gaddis locates the voices of agapistic love, Stephen's dictum of "Dilige et quod vis fac," but reminds readers that they too must be diligent to discern love within the noise of the church's crash at the novel's end. Gaddis's next step is to ask whether love can be heard at all amid the din of contemporaneity that is *J R*.

3 . . . . .
J R

Redemption looks to the small fissure in the ongoing catastrophe.
—*Walter Benjamin, Central Park*

• • • Because the textual complexity of *The Recognitions* posed a formidable challenge to its readership, it is not surprising that most readers were not up to the task; the book's undeserved lack of success meant that Gaddis had to practice his craft in a more practical context. In the twenty years between the publication of *The Recognitions* and the release of *J R*, Gaddis spent time working in industry as a corporate writer, penning publicity for a pharmaceutical firm, creating film scripts for the Pentagon, and writing speeches for business executives. Perhaps as a result of this experience, the vision of reality presented in Gaddis's novel about corporate America presents a more radical challenge to ethics than does *The Recognitions*.

In Gaddis's first novel, the mendacities of capitalism, summarized in Recktall Brown's comment that "money gives significance to anything" (*R* 144), were clearly subordinated to the more fundamental problem of how art, science, and religion can be misconstrued as the locus of virtue. In *J R*, however, Gaddis reminds us that Kant's distinction between "things with dignity" and "things with price" has vanished in a flurry of commodity fetishism. Everything has a price in this world, which is informed by one sacred value—the ethical obligation to make money. As Kemper Fullerton points out, this awareness serves as the foundation of Max Weber's classic study, *The Protestant Ethic and the Spirit of Capitalism*.[1] Weber begins his analysis by citing Benjamin Franklin's "Advice to a Young Tradesman," in which Franklin quotes Proverbs 22, 29: "Seest thou a man diligent in business? He shall stand before kings."[2] This diligence, which Weber argues takes the form of an ethical obligation, stands in direct contrast to the "dilige" of Augustine. Because Jack Gibbs's statement, "can't escape the protestant ethic have to redeem it," serves as the ethical touchstone of this novel, the act of redemption in part requires readers to understand the sacred nature that money has acquired in the world depicted by *J R*.

To do this, readers of *J R* are asked to go beyond the generic Marxist critique of capitalism offered up as the scenario in so many modern and contemporary novels: the fundamental value of human dignity subjected to exploitation, domination, and alienation as a result of class division. This scenario, although painted with a broad brush, is commonplace enough to prompt Frederic Jameson's comment confirming "the privileged status of Marxism as a mode of analysis of capitalism proper."[3] Despite the widespread acceptance of this analysis, however, the Marxist vision is inadequate to the task of accurately representing the complexities of postmodern life present in this novel. *J R* shows readers, as the words of Jean Baudrillard clarify, that things have changed: "The Faustian, Promethean (perhaps Oedipal) period of consumption and production gives way to the 'proteinic' era of networks, the narcissistic and protean era of connection, contact, contiguity, feedback and generalized interface that goes with the universe of communication . . . [and] which leaves far behind those relative analyses of the universe of commodity."[4] *J R* presents readers with a vision of Baudrillard's universe of postmodern capitalism, a world whose superstructure thrives on constant

change and has itself embraced a permanent revolution of capitalist production. As Ernest Mandel points out in *Late Capitalism*,
the standard critique of Marxism—the labor theory of value—is
obsolete in the face of a combination of traditional market anarchy
plus the forces of state intervention wherein the conversion of
everything from raw materials and food to information into commodity has displaced the concept of the social class struggle and
has rendered the vision of the worker's revolution itself into a
helplessly naive fantasy.[5]

Jack Gibbs (through Engels) alludes to this situation when he
succinctly asserts, "The whole God damned problem's the decline
from status to contract" (393, 509, 595). In a decentered world
of globalized commodity fetishism there is no dialectic at work,
no status-based, use value revolutionary aesthetic possible in a
world where there is only contractual exchange value. Schepperman's paintings remain locked up in Zona Selk's country manor,
while composer Edward Bast writes "Zebra Music" for a commercial wildlife film.

In *J R*, then, the expression "*Agapē* agape" does more than
simply entitle character Jack Gibbs's unfinished work; it underscores the conditions that frame the basic question that William
Gaddis's second novel poses to both its characters and readers,
"what's worth doing": how the redemption of an agapistic ethics is
possible, at what cost, and by what means, within the postmodern
capitalism that stands agape at the notion of human dignity.[6]
Answering this question is difficult, especially when one realizes
that Gaddis gives no warrant for belief in conventional aesthetic
solutions. The plot line of *J R* consists of a conflict between two
subtexts—finance and art. In the corporate world of *J R*, where
all monetary worth exists on paper, the shadow of paper instruments has so obscured traditional value structures that depreciation has become the touchstone of worth. Gaddis is not simply
offering commonplace moralizing about the evils of money, how-

ever, because the distorted relationship between means and ends in *J R* is not only monetary but aesthetic. Artists talk incessantly about projects that would redeem their world from venality, but these same artists fail to produce anything worth doing, anything that would confer credibility on their intentions.

Gaddis not only critiques conventional aesthetic solutions within the novel; he sets this critique in a narrative form that dramatizes it. What the novel says about art is mirrored by how the novel says it, creating a form that intractably resists conventional aesthetic means of interpretion. Presented almost entirely in dialogue, *J R* demonstrates what Umberto Eco describes in *The Open Work* as a radical contravention of convention, embodying the radical form of Nietzschean ambiguity that Derrida describes as "the epochal regime of the quotation mark."[7] The dialogue form of *J R* extends the idea that narrative understanding emerges only through an interactive process of negotiation. As it does through the content, the form of *J R* continuously reminds its readers that they will be frustrated as long as they rely on conventional aesthetic means of recovering meaning from it.

Because *J R* offers so little in the way of structural coherence and narrative line, one can sympathize with George Steiner's complaint that "this unreadable book will humiliate, confound, and mock the reader"—sympathize, but not agree.[8] In contrast to Steiner's notion that the unconventional narrative mocks the reader, I would argue that Gaddis creates his "unreadable" text to instruct the reader, offering up a second-order description of the alterity of the world of *J R*. As he did in *The Recognitions*, Gaddis demonstrates this alterity on two levels. Within *J R* the reader finds two competing systems—art and finance—both of which are exposed as fraudulent insofar as they portray singular solutions. Like *The Recognitions*, *J R* both describes the critique of singular structure and enacts it in the form the novel takes. *J R*, however, is more radical in this regard than the previous novel: by eliminating virtually every kind of discursive authorial transition, J R becomes a lonely and problematic read, a narrative in which the mediating guidance of the author is absent. If a reader seeks coherence, repeated readings of J R demonstrate only that meaning and coherence do not constitute intrinsic properties of the text. At the same time, Gaddis also provides readers with the means to engage the first-order virtues of the ethics of indeterminacy, requiring a commitment of risk and responsible suffering in reading this most unconventional narrative to show the reader how to understand in an unconventional way "what's worth doing."

In J R both the method and message of this instruction emerge through the oblique allusions the novel makes to Walter Benjamin. Although I have already drawn a general parallel between Benjamin's and Gaddis's use of collage technique, Benjamin's radical and innovative critique of capitalism serves a more specific function in J R. Like Rilke in *The Recognitions*, Benjamin's presence should not be seen as the constitutive key to unlocking the significance of Gaddis's second novel but rather as the regulative guide that frames Gaddis's presentation.

In his reflections on culture and tradition, Benjamin mirrored Gaddis's belief that in a society dominated by capitalistic institutions the power of art to redeem worth had eroded: The secular cult of beauty and the authenticity of the cultic art work to present it were irrelevant in a world Benjamin saw as a "phantasmagoria" of historicism and the bland culture of progress, a deceptively connected superstructure of "worth" built on the debris and rubble of traditional cultural value.[9] But although Benjamin renounced what he called the "auratic" nature of art, its status as a unique work that could present truth apart from the state and society, he did not reject the role of the artist.[10] Embedded in the ruins of modern culture were thought fragments of truth which survived the perils of progress. In this context the role of the author became an "archaeologist of ruins" whose task was to excavate these fragments, "to wrest the elements of a work from their false context and to reconstruct them in a new one in such a way that the original hidden truth of the work is revealed."[11] Benjamin described this procedure as "politicizing aesthetics," a procedure that did not involve the contemplative artist reassembling value outside society but instead involved the collaborative artist exploiting society's means of production, subverting false structures by illuminating truth through fragments that themselves remained unconnected, ever open to new possibilities of disclosure. In Benjamin's modern world of commodity fetishism, worth no longer exists in the inherent value of the aesthetic object, because the object itself is described by Benjamin as not "in truth."[12] Instead, aesthetic worth becomes synonymous with and contingent on the responsible action of the artist who recovers and displays these fragments. Paralleling quite closely the first-order virtues of risk and responsible suffering that make up Gaddis's ethics of indeterminacy, Benjamin's notion of active collaboration reminds readers of *J R* that what's worth doing becomes in large part the doing itself.

To convey this idea to its reader, *J R* does not preach Benjamin's ideology; instead, Gaddis moves readers from abstract to concrete understanding of this unconventional aesthetic by requiring them to politicize the aesthetics of the novel—to use this view as the means of recovering narrative meaning. Because *J R* molds its language to reflect Benjamin's phantasmagoric world of depreciated value within which are embedded fragments of truth, the reader discovers this method as he works out the linguistic perplexities he encounters, attesting to its tenets by actively engaging in the novel to excavate meaning from it.

Reading *J R* leaves little doubt that any excavation of worth requires diligent spadework; almost every contextual and struc-

tural occurrence in the book is littered with the debris of depreciated and distorted values, both financial and artistic.

Throughout *J R* the distortion of worth by financial community
is symbolized by paper money, a symbol present from the opening
lines of the novel:

> —Money . . . ? in a voice that rustled.
> —Paper, yes.
> —and we'd never seen it. Paper money.
> —We never saw paper money till we came east.
> —It looked so strange the first time we saw it.
> —Lifeless.
> —You couldn't believe it was worth a thing.(1)

These lines suggest two attitudes toward what historians refer
to as "the paper money complex."[13] The first attitude acknowledges an important point in the debate about the relative worth
of coined versus paper money, specifically that paper money was
only a symbol, counted for nothing as a commodity, and was
thus rightly judged to be the worthless material Edward Bast's
aunts deem it to be.[14] In the traditional economic system of
commodity exchange, two types of money, paper and gold, are
clearly disassociated, and it is only the imagination of the capitalist that turns paper "sign" into a valuable substance.[15]

The transference of money's power from the realm of commodity to the realm of the capitalist's imagination is reinforced in
the lines' allusion to a modern version of Wagner's *Das Rheingold*
in which commercial paper has replaced the ring of the Nibelungs
as the source of societal regeneration. To understand this second
allusion, the reader must recall that the opening bars of *The
Rhinegold* consist of a prolonged E-flat in the lower orchestral
register, a sound, Wagner told Liszt, that embraces "The begin-

ning and end of the world."[16] The source of the E-flat and
Wagner's concept of how that tonic might manifest itself in future
generations are most revealing to the present discussion of the
status of paper money in *J R*. Wagner's account of his mental
state when the inspiration for the E-flat motif came to him is as
follows: "I suddenly experienced a feeling as if I were sinking in
swiftly flowing water. Its *rustling* noise soon presented itself as
the musical sound of the E-flat major chord ceaselessly rocking
away in broken figures; these broken figures showed themselves
as melodic passages of increasing movement, but the pure E-flat
major triad never changed and seemed to wish to give the element
in which I stand infinite significance"[17] [italics mine].

Later in life Wagner addressed another power that he also felt
to be protean in its manifestations:

> Though much that is ingenious and admirable has been thought,
> said, and written concerning the invention of money, and of its
> value as an all-powerful cultural force, nevertheless the curse to which
> it has always been subject in song and story should be weighed against
> its praises. There gold appears as the demonic throttler of mankind's
> innocence; so too, our greatest poet [Goethe] has the invention of
> paper money take place as a devil's trick. The chilling picture of the
> spectral ruler of the world might well be completed by the fateful
> ring of the Nibelung as a stock portfolio.[18]

In *J R*'s world the fundamental "rustling chord" Wagner describes is now the rustling voice of paper money described by
Bast's aunts; paper money, as Wagner predicted, has become the
new ring. Similar references to a Wagnerian landscape transformed into a capitalistic Valhalla appear throughout *J R*,
Wagner's theme of the consequences of renouncing spiritual love
for power functioning as the scaffolding for the events in the
novel. In contrast to Wagner's conception of greed as a privation

of love that is doomed to failure, however, the greed in *J R* is Manichean in its manifestations and appears to have thus avoided the Götterdämmerung, the fate that Wagner predicted for a world bereft of love. To this extent, the ring motif in *J R* is less Wagner's and more G. B. Shaw's. As Shaw pointed out in *The Perfect Wagnerite*, he considered the catastrophic close of Wagner's *Ring* an "operatic anachronism."[19] In contrast, Shaw's modernized scenario has Alberich rethink his threat to dethrone Wotan. Instead, Alberich marries into the best Valhalla families and restores his self-respect by succeeding on such a grand scale that he is transformed into a "Krupp of Essen or Carnegie of Homestead," the type of capitalist that Shaw believed would save Europe.[20]

In sum, the ideological significance of the opening lines of the novel combines the tendency of paper money to distort humanity's natural understanding of the relationship between symbol and value with the idea of a capitalistic Alberich, who succeeds in a world without love, to suggest that in this novel the world of finance has transcended the conventional demands and limits of society. Money is sacred, with all of the ritualistic values that such mystification entails.

In *J R*, economic rights are anterior and independent of social ones, the symbol no longer needing justification before a moral tribunal. Capitalists who see things "from a corporate level" (23) do not confuse monetary and moral purpose, a point brought home by the repeated allusions to excrement in the novel. The fact that most business deals in *J R* are conducted in or near toilets and that the prototypical tycoon J R has for his leitmotiv the phrase "Holy Shit" quite deliberately points to Freud's notion of the fetishistic connection between money and feces. With a backward glance to Gaddis's punning point in his first novel *The Recognitions* that reality is Recktall Brown, Gaddis uses money as "Holy Shit" to remind the reader that corporate success involves accepting the pathological and destructive nature of money and acting on it, disregarding any attempt to justify the activity of making money in any moral sense. Free of any sense of social obligation that would involve restriction or sacrifice to a higher good, the corporate world dissolves moral principles into a choice of expediencies. This is the postmodern capitalist world described by Baudrillard and Mandel in which moral belief is absent and economic "shitting" is the only operant force.

To be sure, the consequences of these perverted values are horrific and absurd: the use of radioactive cobalt to make "improved" heads for beer (435), the recycling of condoms as flutes in pianos (532), and the sale of toy weapons to an African revolutionary army, resulting in its annihilation (709). The corporate world is pathological and destructive, Gaddis shows us, because it has totally separated itself from any moral commodity that might restrict its growth. Despite its corrupt nature, however, J R's corporate sensibility is a palpable source of power in contemporary society, and to restore any sense of human value or higher purpose to this society, it becomes clear that this moral bankruptcy must be confronted.

In J R the task of confronting the perversions of corporate America is given to the artists; however, they are not up to the task. To depict the failure of art, Gaddis continues to draw from the Ring, cataloging individual artists as failed, reduced versions of Norse gods. The musician Edward Bast is a bast(ard) and quite possibly an embodiment of both Siegmund and Siegfried, but instead of doing battle with the forces of darkness, Edward is depicted as a slave of corporate business, managing J R's affairs while wasting his musical talent on "Zebra Music" promotional films. Tom Eigen, an author who has written a book much like The Recognitions, is now creatively impotent, a "writer who's run out of agapē" (282), and fellow writer Jack Gibbs's constant refrain, "God damned," serves as Gaddis's comment on the debased spiritual condition of J R's capitalistic Valhalla. The charac-

terizations of artistic failure are later codified by what Gibbs calls
the "türschluss [shut door] syndrome beginning to see the doors
closing all sad words of tongue or pen to see the same God damned
doors Schramm saw closing" (493). Schramm, a painter who
commits suicide, becomes the focus of Gaddis's attacks on the
sensibility of any artist who gives into the *türschluss* syndrome,
a setting in of a "paralysis of will" (492). As Gibbs describes
Schramm's fate: "Problem what happened he always woke up the
same person that went to bed the night before only way he knew
it these God damned words going through his head, go to bed
know he'd wake up the same God damned person finally couldn't
take it anymore, same God damned words waiting for him only
thing to do get rid of the God damned container for the thing
contained, God damned words come around next morning God
damned container smashed on the sidewalk no place for them
to" (283).

The deficiency Schramm exhibits is the same inability to act
that Eigen experienced, a condition where he "finally found everything around him getting so God damned real he couldn't see
straight long enough to write a sentence" (492). Instead,
Schramm, Eigen, and the rest of the artists in *J R* fall victim to
searching for something worth doing, something that forever
eludes each of them and that ultimately destroys Schramm. As
Gibbs tells Eigen later in the novel, Schramm's problem wasn't
sexual impotence; it was spiritual impotence: "Christ look can't
you see it wasn't any of that? It was whether what he was trying
to do was worth doing even if he couldn't do it? Whether anything
was worth writing even if he couldn't write it? Hopping around
trying to redeem the whole God damned thing" (621).

Schramm's penchant for redemption echoes that of Wyatt
Gwyon, the protagonist of *The Recognitions*. In *J R*, however,
Thoreau's doctrine to live deliberately espoused in *The Recogni-
tions* is no longer tenable as an ethical doctrine in the corporate

world. Instead, the doctrine is lampooned, conflated with the idea of making monogrammed doormats (477). Gaddis also recasts Thoreau's doctrine in *Sounds* to "simplify" in the face of a "life frittered away by details" as a slogan of the slithery lawyer, Crawley, reducing the concept to facile encouragement: "And one word of advice, clear your head and get down to one thing. Hello . . .? Yes simplify Mister Bast. Simplify" (449).

Instead of simplifying their world, however, the artists in *J R* are adept only at creating a chaotic life "frittered away by details." Unable to combat the venalities of the corporate world, these artists perceive themselves to be in an entropic state, a condition in which order, as Gibbs lectures his students, is but a convenient fiction, "simply a thin, perilous state we try to impose on the basic reality of chaos" (20). Gaddis further reinforces the notion of order as a perilous condition when Gibbs complains about how impossible it is to communicate with his ex-wife, a complaint that in fact defines what communication theory describes as informational entropy: "whole God damned problem listen whole God damned problem read Wiener on communication, more complicated the message more god damned chance for errors" (483).[21] The chaotic, entropic world of the artist is concretized by the description of the Ninety-sixth Street flat, an enclave, a haven where these artists retreat, ostensibly to create. The reality of the flat, however, is chaos. Crates of "Mazola #24"—the detritus of one of J R's corporations—sully and obscure the artist's texts. All the manuscripts in the flat—Bast's music, Gibbs's and Eigen's writing—are in states of disrepair. As Gibbs describes this chaos, "There's too God damned much entropy going on" (287).

Jack Gibbs should know, because he gives voice to the clearest expression of how impotent artists are in the face of the depreciation of order. Believing that he has leukemia, Gibbs argues that his cancer extends to language, specifically his book, which remains unfinished after sixteen years of work. As Gibbs describes it, "It's like living with an invalid real god damned terminal case, keep hoping he'll pick up his bed and walk like the good book says" (248). Four hundred pages later, however, the reader of *J R* realizes that Gibbs's book will remain both an invalid and an in-valid, incapable of providing an antidote to the toxins of corporate America.

In so describing his work, Gibbs enacts his preciously romantic belief that art cannot flourish in the midst of a chaotic, entropic society. As Gibbs quotes from his book, "All art depends upon exquisite and delicate sensibility and such constant turmoil must be ultimately destructive" (289).

The true reason for this destruction, however, is not the deli-cate and exquisite nature of art so much as it is the failure of the artists in *J R* to recognize that there can be no art until someone makes it, whatever may be the obstacle. The artists intellectualize and complain about the depreciation evident in society yet keep themselves paralyzed by waiting for something worth doing to motivate them.

Because of this paralysis, at the novel's end things change, but they do not improve. Gibbs is still not writing, and as the reader leaves Gibbs, he has been rereading page thirty-five of Hermann Broch's *The Sleepwalkers* for two hours.

Bast retrieves his musical scores from the wastebasket, but unsure of what to do, he stumbles out of the Ninety-Sixth Street flat with Eigen's equivocal advice, "just go and do what you have to," (724) ringing in his ears.

This equivocal stance in the face of impending chaos is not only a condition within the novel; it is enacted by readers con-fronting 726 pages of unmediated, "chaotic" dialogue. As Karl Malmgren has noted, *J R* does not provide the narrative aids present in most works that highlight narrative: clear identification of speakers, description of narrative locale, and provision of dis-cursive transitions.[22] *J R*, in contrast, makes no concessions to fictional continuity; its linguistic patterns never appear to assume coherent narrative patterns because the conventions used to signify such patterns are absent. There are no chapters, no paragraphs, and very few complete sentences in *J R*, the prevailing mark of the novel's idiosyncratic punctuation—the ellipsis—continuing the loose baroque style Gaddis employed in *The Recognitions*. Also missing is the illusion of explicit interchange—A talking to B—because the speakers are never identified and every speaker is interrupted halfway through a statement by the din of other voices competing for the same space on the page. Scenes are not set in *J R*, they occur, and the identification of topics, never mind their relative significance, is left totally to the reader.

What results comes close to capturing the essence of what the linguist C. C. Fries has identified as the form that actual oral dialogue takes.[23] As Fries discovered after analyzing tape recordings of thousands of conversations, the essential aspect of dialogue was the fragment, and the linguistic means of connecting the listener with the speaker of such fragments could not be construed under the rules of grammar at all (Fries refers to them as attention signals). Fries concluded that in factual dialogue there is no such thing as context-free speech, no single utterance that could be set apart and meaningfully analyzed. In other words, the essential nature of fragments and interruptions, together with a lack of exposition, undercuts the basic causal unit of language, the sentence, and thus disallows the tacit assumption of language-generated closure that accompanies the sentence. In Fries's factual world the meaning of language is necessarily connected to the interaction of speakers finishing each other's fragments through an unending process of interpretative construction.

This same interaction operates within *J R*. Its fragments of unending conversation augmented by graphic insertions expose to the reader what Fries suggests is a fallacy of linguistic meaning.[24] Fries explains this fallacy as the mistaken assumption that in whatever dialogue or speech action one engages, the goal is to make conversation at some point unnecessary. The dialogue of J R, however, is not premised on the possibility of closure, does not permit some final collective interpretation apart from the dialogue it ceaselessly speaks. As it does through its content, the form of J R continuously reminds its readers that they will be frustrated as long as they seek some unified, singular meaning from it.

J R does not confine itself to exposing the weakness of art, however, for although it leaves its characters trapped in a conceptual cul-de-sac, the novel also shows the reader the way out. If J R forces readers to realize that conventional wisdom about the efficacy of art is inadequate, the novel also presents them with unconventional wisdom by providing the means to change their role from conceptual analyst to experiential participant, a role that teaches that it is their own collaboration that imparts significance to the text. The first clue is provided by Jack Gibbs's unfinished work entitled "something agape I think it was" (282), or as the reader later discovers, "*agapē* agape" (605). Gibbs's book "about random patterns and mechanization" (147) is not a novel but "more of a book about order and disorder more of a social history of mechanization and the arts, the destructive element" (244). Gibbs identifies this element as the problem of eliminating failure; democracy's promise, reviving a term used in *The Recognitions*, is "to banish failure to inherent vice" (571): "shoot the God damned piano that's what it's about just told you, player piano play by itself get to shoot the pianist just read it God damn it says it right here, here where the invention was eliminating the very possibility of failure as a condition for success" (604). To the careful reader, Gibbs's statements suggest several points. Gibbs acknowledges that the theme of his book is explicitly related to Oscar Wilde's notion of the relationship of democracy, technology, and art. Paraphrasing Wilde, Gibbs ironically notes that the "frail human element [which] still abounded even in the arts" was usurped by the "saving grace" of the machine: "deliverance was at hand, born of the beasts with two backs called arts and sciences whose rambunctious coupling came crashing the jealous enclosures of class, taste, and talent, to open the arts to Americans for democratic action and leave history to bunk" (289). The thematic concerns of the agency of the artist and the influence of technology on art also allude, in an oblique way, to two works more pertinent to the themes of random patterns and mechanization in the arts, Walter Benjamin's essays, "The Work of Art in the Age of Mechanical Reproduction" and "The Destructive Character."[25] The connection is far greater than merely a similarity in phrasing between these titles and the subject of Gibbs's book, however, for Gaddis uses Benjamin in J R to teach readers how failure can function as the necessary precondition for success, specifically for the recovery of an understanding of what's worth doing in J R.

Benjamin's status is enigmatic: He is a Marxist critic whose theories, as Christopher Norris describes them, "are rife with contradiction and paradox but freed from the narrowing rationalist dogma" of "enlightened" Marxist thinking, which Benjamin saw drawing a too facile equation between knowledge and progress.[26] Instead, Benjamin formulated a fitful kind of Marxism incorporating a catastrophist philosophy of history in which beliefs are kept alive precisely by renouncing progress and history. The present world, Benjamin argues, is lost to truth, for history is always written by the oppressors of true enlightenment. In modernity Benjamin saw the oppressor as capitalism, "a natural phenomenon with which a new dreaming sleep came over Europe and with it a reactivation of mythical forces,"[27] in this instance the forces of technology, commodity fetishism, and the distorted social relationships they generated. Like the younger Marx, Benjamin's aim was waking the world from its dream about itself.

What is needed to change this situation is not simply a worker's revolution, as conventional Marxism holds, but a total revolution, a revolution of consciousness.

These tendencies crystallize in "The Work of Art in the Age of Mechanical Reproduction," in which Benjamin discusses the impact of technological changes and social transformations on aesthetic perception and the modes of aesthetic production. In modern society Benjamin identified reality as artifice: an amalgam of commodities and architectural construction made possible by industrialization. Benjamin stressed that this artifice was nature, a concrete realization (in concrete) of society's dream rather than simply a reified expression of that dream. In an industrialized world of commodity production art, too, has become a commodity with what Benjamin termed exhibition value, the shock of the new that was the province of mass-produced art. The socioeconomic realities of the twentieth century had demonstrated to Benjamin the bankruptcy of the aesthetic approach as a means of ideological intervention: the power of money and capitalism being far too pervasive to be transformed by any intellectual love of beauty. But if the emergence of the exhibition value of art led to a crisis in aesthetic perception, it also left open the possibility for emancipation, allowing art to move from the realm of shopworn ideas and cathartic experiences to a realm of critical cultural argument. In such a climate, the task of the artist became not to represent the artifice that had become reality but to expose to people how and why artifice had become reality. Benjamin described this as the movement from "aestheticizing politics" (raising the mundane to art, for Benjamin the essence of Fascism) to "politicizing aesthetics," reviving art in the twentieth century by acknowledging its status as a product, then integrating the means of production with human concerns through collaborative activity.[28]

To understand this approach more clearly, consider Benjamin's use of the thought fragment technique in his *Theses on the Philosophy of History*, a sequence of eighteen aphoristic statements that, although nominally pessimistic, can also be read as redemptive parables, what Adorno called Benjamin's goal of presenting "the paradox of the possibility of the impossible."[29] The *Theses* critiques belief in any historical system—including Marxist historical materialism—that equates the goal of history with the end of time. In rejecting teleology as a basis for understanding, however, Benjamin also affirms the messianic belief in the illumination of truth in the moment, an illumination provided by the fragments that compose the *Theses*, wherein theory suddenly stops "in a configuration pregnant with tensions."[30] In such fragmentary configurations one sees the chance, as Benjamin describes it throughout the *Theses*, to displace a specific moment of truth from the otherwise banal and homogeneous course of history.

The same concern with fragments also seems to inform Gibbs's writing. Apart from his citations from Wilde, Gibbs exhibits a fascination with epigraphs. Listed on page 486 of *J R* and reproduced below, the thematic link among these epigraphs parallels Benjamin's focus on the dual themes of human desolation and utopian ideals. Gibbs describes the quotations as "mere trash," but Gaddis's purpose of turning the reader into a Benjamin-like collaborator is nonetheless strengthened by their presence. Gibbs asks Amy, "What are there about a dozen?" (487), but in fact there are eighteen, the same number as in Benjamin's *Theses*. (Although nineteen are listed in *J R*, the fourteenth duplicates the second.) The point is not to compare the two sets of thought fragments directly but rather to note the possibility of recognizing in *J R* the same formal and thematic concerns found in Benjamin. Quotations in *J R* more directly related to Benjamin's concept of thought fragments are found on page 587, also reproduced here. The reader finds in Gibbs's notes a mirror of Benjamin's basic themes: socioeconomic upheaval (the depression, union

The unswerving punctuality of chance
A bat as a mouse's idea of an angel
How less like anyone we can be than unlike ourselves
A friendliness, as of dwarfs shaking hands, was in the air
The total depravity of inanimate things (E.M.FORSTER)

Taine's 'Le con d'une femme' as the axis round which everything
    turns
Who uses whom? (LENIN)?)

Of the soul being set before its Maker hatless, disheveled
    and free with its spirit unbroken (K. MANSFIELD)

To see clearly and be able to do nothing (HERACLITUS)

~~As if the roots of the earth were rotten, cold and drenched~~ (KEATS)

Lady Brute: that may be an error in the translation
Growing up as a difficult thing which few survive
                      (HEMINGWAY?)

Life as what happens to us while we are busy making other plans
The melancholia of things completed
His heart yearning towards the defeated enemy now subject,
    at his free choice, to be spared or killed, and therefore never
    so lovely (T.E. LAWRENCE)

Pascal's being less unlike others than we can be unlike
    ourselves
Beware women who blow on knots
That a work of art has a beginning, middle and end,
    life is all middle
There is a saying, if any stranger enquire of the first met of
    Maan, were it even a child, "Who is here the sheykh?"
    he would answer him, "I am he" (C.M. DOUGHTY, TRAVELS
    IN ARABIA DESERTA)

~~It is true that in the heights of enthusiasm I have been~~
  ~~cheated into some fine passages, but~~
Gogol's character who in the end became a kind of gaping
    hole in humanity

1920
ex PPC 32, 34, 83, 87H, 137-9, 143:4

1920

1920
the Sackbut London vln2 The Pianola as a Means of Personal
                              Expression / Alvin Langdon Coburn
He holds that it is an instrument for the artist, 2hrs practice a
day for a year to master it. Its deadliest enemy the mediocre pianist
Diff frm gramophone whose records are invariable perfs (pianola's
fingers drop 1/2") "the arts must accept the new conditions and make
the most of them"

23rd US depression since 1790 (6/1/23)   O Little Town of B'hem
HFord's antiSemitic campaign war65ff/K5   That old Irish Mother of mine
        Mah-jongg rep (depression)   Holst's The Planets
    RUR (Eng trans 1923)   Caruso last appnce   Elgar 'Enigma Variations' Js

1920 Lasky had got to Hollywood to combat hostility of dramatic critics
& littérateurs toward movies Maeterlinck Maugham Grtrude Atherton EGlyn
arrived there in 1920 'It did not take the authors long to discover
their presence in Hwood was only windowdressing' they left angry sorry
"Maeterlinck's first scenario was 'a charming little tale about a small
boy who discovered some fairies. I'm afraid (wrote Mr Samuel Goldwyn)
my reactions to it were hardly fairy-like.'" (n /92/? v. VMC)
EGlyn of Valentino: Do you know he had never even though t of kissing
the palm, rather than the back, of a woman's hand until I made him do it!

downgrading music ed. standards (democratising) LEM58 - musician as menace,
                                              one-sided ec. LEM63
  1,060,858 children between 10-15 in US gainfully high ideals 735
    employed :mfrng & mech industries 185,337; textiles 54,649
      B.Gigli debut in Boito's Mefistofele   College Boards too tough,
  KDKA Pittsburgh first regular radio broadcasting srvice dropped-LEM163
  Dame Nellie Melba sang over radio at Chelmsford Eng; hrd in Persia "167
      5000 replies in 05   art for art sake obsolete -192
  NY Wall st bomb exp WA141 committed OY59 34 music teachers 130,265 "198
  Sacco-Vanzettiaccused in murder WA141 also 1921, 27
  Ponzi-144AF arrest 149 demonstrations abroad OY68 Sec. of Fine Arts LEM60
  Gaston B.Means joins Justice dept. NF151   1920s - 1950 perfectionism
  employees militantly on union see Case & Boston   passé- 61
      'American Plan' (est gun shop, promoted Symph. " music ed 186
  total 3411 strikes   destroy unanism   " music conditioning
                                              cf. Pavlov 203

  NYrs day A Mitchell Palmer arrests cmmnsts FLA40 & union tieins
    Reed as a cmmnst leadr was indicted in absentia, in Russia in
    fact where though he tried to get home died age 33 typhus lay in
    state fr a week in Moscow's trade union center   hurt musicians
  top b.s. The Man of the Forest Zane Grey (this side of Paradise Main) 1st amendment
  Qs voted for first time in 1920 election- helped put across prohibition
  Al Capone signs up with Torrio in Chicago (M.I)   as foundation for
  ATcT patent agreements USPS 73 dial phone introduced OY174-79 of 83
  Wilson run from unanimity USPS278   own finances
  SKW essay on Fed Sedition Law (p67)   Man o' War 2min 14 1/5 sec
    Ford 1a minute KS42 Ford income KS284   1 3/8 mi stretch-Belmont
  Divorce rate 13.4 per hundred marriages OY51 Chicago White Sox
  Mayakovsky- another poem t himself Bd137   Chicago theatre strike
    prizefighting legalized in NY (Walker Xn senate)

conflicts, child labor), the failure of traditional art (rejection of artists by film industry), and especially the need to politicize aesthetics ("Art for art's sake obsolete"; "the arts must accept the new conditions and make the most of them").

Art is certainly understood to have exhibition value in *J R*, a value expressed by Major Hyde when he tells Gibbs where art comes from: "Get it? Art? You get it where you get anything you buy it. . . . don't try and tell me in this day and age there isn't enough around for everybody great art, picture music books who's heard all the great music there is you? You read all the great books there are? seen all these great pictures? records of any symphony you want reproductions you can get them that are almost perfect, the greatest books ever written you can get them at the drugstore" (48). In Hyde's corporate world of perverted values, art has become a commodity of "drugstore masterpieces," part of what Gibbs describes as the "God damned Protestant ethic can't escape it have to redeem it" (477). The means of redemption, as Gibbs tells Amy, requires the type of change Benjamin advocated, a change of contexts: "I mean sometimes there are situations that just don't seem to have a solution in their own context do you, do you see what I mean? And the only way to, the only thing to do is step in and change the whole context" (496). Although Gibbs cannot act on his own advice, his remarks provide important clues to the reader. Because *J R* exhibits the distorted structures and bankrupt values of capitalism described by Benjamin and because the novel resists conventional aesthetic interpretation, the task of the reader is to blast from the bunk of the novel's encrusted contexts of false value fragments that illuminate an understanding of worth heretofore hidden.

In this context, *J R*'s allusions to Hermann Broch's *Sleepwalkers* are revealing (629, 724). As discussed earlier, Broch believed the role of art was to reveal the means by which man could recover a sense of value in a fragmented world. By radically revising narrative style to mirror discoveries in the new physics,

Broch created what he called epistemological novels in which the active participation of the reader in constructing meaning became the primary issue. Jack Gibbs gives voice to this idea when he states "don't bring a God damned thing to it can't take a God damned thing from it don't know something look it up" (605). Ironically, the fact that Jack Gibbs has been reading page thirty-five of the *Sleepwalkers* for two hours is stark testimony that he is unable to act on his own advice, will never junk his failed aesthetic sensibility to do the hard work necessary to get to page 648, and so will never hear what Broch describes in the last lines of the novel as "the voice of man and of the tribes of men, the voice of comfort and hope and immediate love: 'Do thyself no harm! For we are all here!' "[31] In reading the epistemological novel *J R*, the reader faces the same dilemma: either participate in the construction of the text's meaning or else be condemned to endlessly read *J R*'s "same page" of verbal noise. The allusion to Broch underscores what the allusions to Benjamin point out. Rather than try to aestheticize the paper-money world of the novel as the artists of the novel try and fail to do, the reader can politicize aesthetics, take art into the world of action by carefully considering oblique allusions—indirect and therefore more valuable—as possible sources for illuminating what's worth doing in *J R*.

Examined carefully, *J R* yields a series of intricate connections concerning fragments in the complementary context Benjamin accords them, connections that aid the reader in the understanding and experience of politicizing aesthetics. For example, early in *J R* there is an expressed concern over an inscription engraved in the front of Gibbs's school. The inscription resists translation, although Gibbs drops some hints to the reader that it might be from Empedocles: "I think it's a fragment from the second generation of his cosmology, maybe even from his first" (45). The reference to Empedocles seems to satisfy most characters in the novel. Later, however, the reader finds that Schepperman, the painter, engraved it, an engraving Gibbs describes as one of Schepperman's attempts to make a statement that people could see: "Schepperman God damned statements still got one of his God damned statements carved in stone over the God damned front door, God damned school board find it's Karl Marx" (409). Disguised by little curlicues added to the letters (457), the statement is indeed a fragment, but it is not from Empedocles. Turning back to the fragments on page twenty, if readers shift their perspective, they can recognize the obscured letters of "from each according to. . . ." The implications are complex and fascinating.

By first providing a supposed reference to Empedocles, himself a believer in destruction as the precondition for meaning (actual fragments of Empedocles's _Fragments_ appear on pages 45, 161, and 406), Gaddis nudges the reader into discovering the real significance of the quotation. The reference to Marxism (from each according to his ability, to each according to his need) reminds the reader that systems opposing J R's capitalistic money game can exist. More importantly, however, the reference reinforces the significance of Walter Benjamin's messianic transcience, his vitalist revision of Marxist materialism that in the context of reading J R means actively engaging the novel's verbal means of production, taking on fragments such as Schepperman's that the reader himself must wrench into a previously undisclosed context that confers meaning.

This technique is particularly useful when applied to the subject of entropy, which as previously mentioned appears to symbolize a predetermined state of inevitable chaos that permeates both the lives of the artists in the novel and the reader's attempts to structure it. In so viewing such chaos, however, Gibbs, Eigen, and the nonattentive reader miss Gaddis's covert message that entropy is not determined, not a function of the cosmos, but is instead a result of choices humans themselves make about the possibility of order. Two fragments from *J R* corroborate this interpretation of entropy's function in the novel.

First, the name Jack Gibbs may well be a reference to Josiah Willard Gibbs, the nineteenth-century American physicist/chemist so beloved and misunderstood by Henry Adams.[32] Jack Gibbs's negative interpretation of entropy, although in line with Adams's idea of the heat death of the universe, is at odds with Willard Gibbs's own pronouncements on the subject. Specifically, when Willard Gibbs established probability as a fundamental concept of physics, he was not reducing the concept of significant ordered action to the perilous condition Jack Gibbs describes to his class. Instead, Willard Gibbs revised the relationship between order and disorder, suggesting that "the impossibility of an uncompensated decrease of entropy seems to be reduced to improbability,"[33] that irreversibility of increasing disorder was not a given. The clearest explanation of Gibbs's idea was put forth by scientist E. T. Jaynes. Noting the usefulness of Gibbs's formulations, Jaynes declared "that even at the purely phenomenological level, entropy is an anthropomorphic concept. For it is a proposition, not of the physical system, but of the particular experiments you or I choose to perform on it."[34] Willard Gibbs provided the insight that entropy is not an independent entity threatening humanity's existence but an anthropomorphic tool that offers answers, especially in the application of thermodynamics to chemistry, unforeseen in antecedent theories.

The second fragment concerns the reader's willingness to take seriously Jack Gibbs's suggestion to "read Wiener on communication" (403), referring to Norbert Wiener, a pioneer in the field of cybernetics (the theory of codes and their discernment within a state of informational entropy).[35] When Jack Gibbs complains about the possibility of increased error in complicated messages, he underscores the relationship between complexity and unpredictability in communication. However, Jack Gibbs leaves out the other side of the coin of information theory: the more recognizable the message, the more banal and predictable it is, in effect replacing error with emptiness. More importantly, Jack Gibbs fails to consider what information theory proposes as the way out of this dilemma, the human mind, a point Wiener stresses throughout his work. Through the intermediary of past experience, a priori knowledge is available about the message and its symbols. This knowledge generates feedback, which both reduces the uncertainty of the message and allows new and unexpected interpretations to take place. As did Willard Gibbs, Wiener sees entropy not simply as an outside force acting on humanity but as one that includes humanity as an agent endeavoring to interfere with the natural random order of events. Wiener goes on to equate information and value as "negative entropy," the motive force in the relationship of humans to their environment, for in seeking order and knowledge people continually try to establish an otherwise improbable congruence between human ideas and natural events. Because of the possibility of what he called "local enclaves of order," Wiener felt that the randomness associated with entropy was a privation, an Augustinean "organic incompleteness" rather than the "positive malicious evil of the Manichaeans": "the Augustinean devil, which is not a power in itself, but the measure of our own weakness, may require our full resources to uncover, but when we have uncovered it, we have in a certain sense exorcised it, and it will not alter its policy on a matter already decided with the mere intention of confounding us further."[36] In presenting entropy as a thought fragment that, when placed in a new context, can be understood as something other than an indication of absolute disorder, Gaddis asks the reader to go beyond the confines of the deterministic action within the text. Having shown us "What America's all about, waste disposal and all" (27), Gaddis is requiring that readers dispose of the novel's waste by stretching their ability to meet the need and redeem an implausible order within an otherwise entropic novel.

In sum, Gaddis's use of Benjamin in both the form and content of J R first provides the sense that art is bankrupt as long as it stands apart from the socioeconomic realities of the world of late capitalism. Second, Benjamin's theory provides a vision of the reader as a collaborator who pieces together the fragments of artistic insight to circumvent conventional and distorted wisdom about the very possibility of order.

One should not assume that the novel simply replicates a messianic Marxism, however, for Benjamin's thought-fragments technique applies as well to another source of establishing worth buried under the debris of J R's corporate world. Returning again to Jack Gibbs's book as a source for fragments, the careful reader recalls Gibbs's comment to Amy that the book is "about a lot of things its can't say what a book's about before it's done that's what any book worth reading's about, problem solving" (499). To solve the problem of establishing coherent meaning within J R, the reader must examine another "thing" discussed in Gibbs's book, the concept "as another mother country throwback had it, [that] all art does constantly aspire to the condition of music" (289). This reference to Walter Pater's concept of the position of music as the highest art form, together with the opening sentence of Gibbs's book, "Music is free to all" (203), suggests that the reader take Gibbs's ideas about random patterns and relate them to the musical references in J R.

In so doing, one finds that it is not true, as one critic put it, that "there is no music in J R";[37] the problem is to discern its tonic and overtones amid the cacophony the novel presents. The problem is solved if one returns to the Wagnerian fundamental tonic of E-flat, considering it not in its transfigured monetary form that opens the novel but in its original state, which can effect a kind of Keatsian "negative capability" in an audience.

As Bast tells Amy, "No not asking them making them, like that E-flat chord that opens the *Rhinegold* goes on and on for a hundred and thirty-six bars until the idea that everything's happening under water is more real than sitting in a hot plush seat with tight shoes on" (111).

The means by which one understands the potential transformational power of music as represented by the E-flat tonic is the confusion between Wagner and Mozart in *J R*. As a result of mixing up instructional tapes at J R's school, the reader hears characters mentioning Mozart's *Ring* ("Mozart's Rhinegold," 29; "Mozart's, ah, Ring, is it?" 39). At first, this confusion seems only to confirm the chaotic and worthless instruction taking place at the school. Investigated more carefully, however, this confusion between the two composers reveals an important linkage concerning how to recover meaning within a chaotic landscape, the concept of *agapē*.

In *Mozart, His Character His Work*, Alfred Einstein notes that Mozart's last opera, *The Magic Flute*, was written in the same E-flat key Wagner used in the *Ring*.[38] By itself, this fact is not extraordinary, because on the surface there seems to be little similarity between Mozart's innocuous libretto about the fortunes of Tamino and Wagner's cosmic myths. Einstein goes on to say that E-flat is the masonic key, however, and that *The Magic Flute* was designed by Mozart as a tribute to the ethical tenets of freemasonry, specifically the concern with the alleviation of man's fear of death by teaching him the selfless, cosmic principle of *agapē*.[39] To overcome the fear of personal extinction that underlies the fear of death, the Masons taught that man should neither deny death nor try to escape its consequences. Instead, one must embark upon a chthonic journey to hell itself, shedding personal concern to reach the intellectual illumination that death is nothing to fear because individual identity is not important. This recognition leads one to the condition of *agapē*, an acceptance of selflessness that paradoxically frees one for the experience of living life, not by amassing wealth or holding power, but by giving, by caring for others more than for oneself.

One can now understand the concept of Mozart's *Ring* in a new way, as an oblique allusion to the concept of *agapē*. Already conspicuous by its repeated mention in such an otherwise loveless book, *agapē* can now be understood as Gaddis's specific alternative to the greed and inaction present within the novel. With a backward glance at the "Holy Shit" of money, the reader is better able to understand Gaddis's frequent reference to a letter written by Mozart in which he says that "believing and shitting are two very different things" (42). Mozart recognized the necessity of the "shit" of money, as Gaddis reminds us through numerous references to the composer's money problems (40–42). As Mozart's letter reminds us, however, belief is a different state, a way of achieving the higher truth dramatized by Mozart's music, as long as one clearly separates belief from greed and the worship of money.

Gaddis does not confine this oblique allusion to Mozart and his work. Within the novel, the reader now has a better understanding of why Gaddis made James, Bast's uncle and a "genius" composer according to the otherwise cynical Gibbs (117), a member of the masonic order (11, 62). Genius, music, and *agapē* are equated throughout *J R*. If one explores carefully, one finds that Wagner, the composer mentioned most often in *J R*, shifted his spiritual allegiance from Feuerbachian Eros to Schopenhauerian *agapē*, a belief quite similar to Mozart's: namely, that one reaches illumination through a journey wherein people confront and let go of their individuality on the way to a higher state of consciousness.[40] Beethoven, an ardent admirer of *The Magic Flute*, likewise practiced the fundamental tenet of freemasonry, a belief that informs Gibbs's use of a quotation from the deaf composer that "the better of us keep one another in mind" (290).[41] Even Gibbs's gloomy philosopher, Empedocles, posited a form of love similar to _agapē_ as the principle that would musically transform the strife, the Benjamin-like fragments of the world, into order.[42]

The oblique allusions to _agapē_ share a cosmic vision. Suffering, randomness, and chaos are the unavoidable conditions of life that can neither be controlled by money nor refined out of existence by art. By living according to the selfless principle of _agapē_, however, one can transform this chaos. The world is entropic, but in the way Willard Gibbs rather than Jack Gibbs suggested: a random system in which order is improbable but not impossible. Faced with the shut door, the _türschluss_ syndrome, the reader now has the key to open it.

Armed with this knowledge, the reader can now better understand Jack Gibbs's comment that his fellow failed artist, Thomas _Eigen_ (self or own, in German) had "run out of agapē." As Rhoda reminds Bast, Schramm's suicide was not a result of despair. Like the other artists in _J R_, Schramm couldn't use his aesthetic gift as a means of redemption because he could not get away from his ego: "None of you trust anybody you're all scared shitless of it [passion and intimacy] aren't you, I mean he's so hung up on this book he's scared to lose this lousy opinion of himself that's why none of you can" (606). Gibbs interrupts at this point, but Gaddis's point is made nevertheless. By focusing on the self, Schramm and the other artists in _J R_ ironically perpetuate the very tendency of contemporary society to eliminate failure as the precondition for success that Gibbs finds so abhorrent. As long as artists remain concerned with avoiding the failure of self-destruction, none of them can reach the state of _agapē_, the only state by which the chaos of society can be successfully transformed.

The ethical tenet that emerges from _J R_ is, as Edward reminds the reader, in the doing: "I mean until a performer hears what I hear and can make other people hear what he hears it's just trash"

(724). The crux, of course, is to play this music in the no deposit, no return world of *J R*, where the possibility of failure to do anything is great.

Offering an insight strikingly similar to the allusions to Rilke that appear in *The Recognitions*, the parabolic allusions to Benjamin and *agapē* in *J R* provide another means for the reader to become a collaborator in the text, assembling the *plumpes denken* (Benjamin's "crude thought") that refer to *agapē* so that the reader can transform the apparent narrative chaos of *J R* into meaning. Although sharing the strength of Rilke's transformational vision, however, *J R* extends the idea of creating the experience of recovering meaning from a world of essential indeterminacy through its use of dialogue, a dialogue considered as interaction between the reader and the text rather than between characters.

In using dialogue to give the reader the direct experience of recovering meaning from an indeterminate text, Gaddis draws from a tradition going back to the Greeks.[43] One recalls that Socratic dialogue involves not simply interrogation, but also dialectical questioning, an interchange in which each participant's own conceptual barriers are called into question. Through this partial negation of concept, a transformation of understanding takes place. Dialogic understanding approximates experiential understanding in that knowledge is not gained through reflection. Instead, dialogue is an activity, a breaking down and breaking open of old ways of seeing.

But if dialogue is the linguistic form best suited to breaking down and breaking open conceptual barriers so that one can actually experience new horizons of understanding, how is it that a text like *J R* can be understood to question readers, to engage them in the same way participants in an oral dialogue can? The fact that the novel is composed entirely of dialogue does not answer this question; simply presenting its characters as talking with each other is totally inadequate to capturing the experiential nature of oral dialogue in written form. The great difficulty involved in writing this sort of dialogue is that the very nature of the printed word takes language from a realm of interchange to a realm of monologue. In any writing, the author has created a text and left it; there is no immediacy of contact, no possibility of mutual monitoring that helps to shape communication in oral discourse. In written discourse it seems, as Jacques Lacan puts it, that "there is no such thing as dialogue, it is a swindle."[44]

Focusing on the dialogue of *J R*, however, one realizes that it does not cheat the reader. To circumvent the restriction of inevitable authorial absence, to provide a means by which a reader and the text can talk to each other, *J R* can be understood as a dissonant dialogue, in the sense that Nietzsche meant when he described the Dionysian state that subverts the harmonious Apollonian ideal to reveal tragedy's informing insight that all ideal appearance is illusory.[45] Although it subverts ideals, the larger significance of dissonance is that it enables one not only to encounter but to endure this disillusionment through the opportunities for creative response and judgment it offers. Although Nietzsche confined his discussions of the technique of dissonance to music (like Gaddis, Nietzsche greatly admired Wagner and what he called the enthusiasm of Mozart's dance), the idea also fits *J R*, because like its dissonant musical cousins this novel leaves out key "notes" whose presence would otherwise insure a harmonious resolution at some level.

When considered earlier, dialogue was discussed as Gaddis's way of blunting aesthetic closure. Because it does not identify voices, provide causally connected sequences, or clarify speakers' contexts, the unedited dialogue of *J R* lacks the traditional means by which readers find help in understanding texts unmediated by the author. Although removing meaning and continuity as intrinsic properties of the text, the dissonant dialogue of *J R* also points to the creation of a different type of narrative activity in which the meaning of a text is a product of the activities performed on it by readers who "hear" what the text has to say, then "speak" back to questions the text poses. Historically, dialogue takes as its premise that truth emerges only when it is forced, a condition Bakhtin describes as anacrisis, the scene of making the other speak.[46] J R promotes this kind of activity by enforcing the reader's intimacy with both the character and events of the novel.

In J R, the speaker at any particular time is not specified. Because of this omission, readers can sort out individual speakers only by listening, as Malmgren notes, for recurrent linguistic idiosyncrasies and assigning them to various characters.[47] As previously explained, the presence of Jack Gibbs is signaled by the expression "God damned," while J R's repeating motifs are "hey" and "Holy Shit." Mr. Whiteback, school principal and bank president, is identified by the "ahm" that pervades his rambling commentary. Rhoda, resident prostitute at the Ninety-sixth Street flat, is distinguished by her affection for the hippie idiom "like," and Governor Cates demonstrates a predilection for the imperative mood. Because readers are never told through the dissonant dialogue who these characters are, they must adapt themselves to the idea that they are supposed to know the who, where, and when of the characters through intimate knowledge of the sound of their voices. To the reader's question, "Who is talking now?" the text will only reply, "The person right next to you."

The intimacy enforced by the dissonant dialogue disturbs the reader who expects at some narrative level a delineation of fictive roles. The experience of reading J R shatters these expectations and forces the reader to realize that the characters simply cannot be identified by traditional narrative means. Readers, in other words, have come to experience the boundaries of their conceptual awareness of the novel. In so doing, they also take the first step in engaging the text as dialogue. Unable to interrogate characters conceptually, readers must engage in something easily forgotten in the lust for closure. Within the perceived dissonance of *J R*, they must, as J R reminds them in the last lines of the novel, listen: "So I mean I got this neat idea, hey, you listening. Hey? You listening . . . ?" (726).

But listening, as Thoreau reminds us in *Wednesday*, is only half of the process of dialogue: It takes two to speak the truth—one to speak and another to hear. The other half involves speaking, responding to the comments and queries of the questioner. In a novel in which so much of the heard speech occurs on the telephone, this means that the reader who speaks to J R does so by supplying the other half of the phone conversations, assembling the fragments of information scattered among J R's purchase orders (J R uses the phone to disguise the fact that he is eleven years old), Cates's harangue about business deals, or Whiteback's feeble attempts at diplomacy to provide some context of meaning in which the reader can answer back. What is being said and for what purpose is known only if the reader creates the context for the conversation; otherwise, the conversations intermingle and disappear. That this process cannot be illustrated by providing representative examples attests to how scattered and disconnected are the fragments that the reader must assemble to create these contexts. One cannot simply read a critical article about *J R* to grasp this; one must listen and speak to the 726 pages of the novel.

By being required both to listen and speak to the text to recover narrative meaning, the reader can draw the conclusion that *J R* is not simply a text for interpretation but is also a book about interpretation, an interpretation of interpretation. Because the dissonant dialogue of the novel demands a narrative interaction wherein the reader must listen to the voices of the characters and must create the contexts for their speeches, one can say that *J R* speaks, uses language to help the listening reader realize that understanding and active experience are inseparable. Through the dissonance of its dialogue, *J R* insists again and again that its meaning exists neither as formal understanding that precedes its reading nor as a conceptual understanding arising from its reading; rather, meaning exists as an experiential understanding inseparable from the act of collaborative interpretation. In recalling the last word spoken to him by a dying patient, Bast reminds the reader how collaborative action can simultaneously confer worth: "I never had to, it was just something I'd never questioned before I thought it was all I was here for and he, everybody thought that they thought that I was doing something worth doing he did too but he, nothing's worth doing he told me nothing's worth doing till you've done it and then it was worth doing even if it wasn't because that's all you . . . " (715). By cutting off Bast at this point, Gaddis reminds the reader that amid the chaos of contemporary life, action itself is, in effect, all that humans have to confirm "that's all you." As Gibbs reminds Eigen, Schramm committed suicide because he kept searching for some touchstone of value and meaning apart from the act of creating, kept wondering "whether what he was trying to do was worth doing even if he couldn't do it? Whether anything was worth writing even if he couldn't write it?" (621). *J R* provides the answer that worth, meaning, and value exist only when one is creating, that action alone is what bestows worth.

In making meaning indistinguishable from action, the specific phenomenology of the event of textual interpretation mirrors the general phenomenology of understanding as explained by the ethics of indeterminacy. In both talking and listening to *J R*, the reader and the book become one system, as unspecifiable and unpredictable as subatomic particles. Like the absolute uncertainty that informs quantum mechanics, Gaddis's dissonant dialogue in *J R* demonstrates that no formula exists that can predict in advance of experience the actual consequences of reader / book interaction. And as quantum physics helps scientists cope with indeterminate states, dissonant dialogue helps readers face the absence of a determining formula for human actions. When one confronts a bewildering set of circumstances, one neither submits these circumstances to a priori formulas nor despairs that they are meaningless; instead, one transforms them, generating meaning within an indeterminate, complementary landscape through collaborative interpretation.

To insure that any recovery of meaning is contingent on action the reader takes, J R does not emphasize any subject, instead presenting good music and bad money with equal amounts of evidence. The recurring image of the pianola, the "refurbished" larynx of the dead singer (288), and the graphic equivalence of the J R corporate logo—the dollar sign—and the musical clef (536) suggests that money and music can be connected in the attempt to "get the God damned artist out of the arts once and for all" (288). The shit, as Gaddis reminds us, can be left in the piano (142). What separates the two subjects is humans acting, striving to transform fragments into meaning by being willing to give up the self, to listen.

Gaddis draws out the implications of not acting in this way by reminding the reader how easily art can be reduced to an abbreviated shorthand culture for the masses. As was seen in Gibbs's description of his book as a terminally ill patient, the only clearly metaphorical artistic descriptions in the book are negative, specifically suggesting that as long as art is static, encapsulated in ready-made tropes passively perceived, it is banal. The metaphors in J R do not present love as *agapē* but rather as Coach Vogel's love circuitry, a metaphor that depicts the act of love as the mindless thrill of an electric shock: "Micro Farad yes that's farad's an electrical unit, his resistance at a minimum and his field fully excited, laid Millie Amp on the ground potential, raised her frequency and lowered her capacitance, pulled out his high voltage probe and inserted it into her socket connecting them in parallel, and short circuited her shunt . . . —bar magnet had lost all its field strength, Millie Amp tried self-induction and damaged her solenoid" (329–30). Such comedic metaphorical debasement of values such as love is reinforced at the end of the novel, when the reader finds that MAMA (Modern Allies of Modern Art) is going to court to prevent the destruction of a contemporary sculpture that has a little boy hopelessly trapped inside it. Gaddis satirizes the Museum of Modern Art's emphasis on business rather than life, for the little boy is trapped, according to a press release, to prevent "the willful destruction of a unique metaphor of man's relation to the universe," a sculpture that goes "beyond conventional limits of beauty to celebrate in the virile and aggressive terms of raw freedom the triumphant dignity of man" (672).

J R himself has already voiced his disbelief in any intangible quality art may possess by describing the experience of listening to Bach's *Cantata 21* as follows: "Okay, okay! I mean what I heard first there's all this high music right? So then this here lady starts singing up yours so then this man starts singing up mine up mine, then there's some words so she starts singing up mine up mine so he starts singing up yours up yours so then they go to back and forth like that up mine up yours up mine up yours that's what I heard?" (658).

This reduction of music is continued by Vogel, now a doctor at Ray-X Corporation, who is busily trying to perfect his frozen shard technique of freezing sounds, including the "old classics in music," then later thawing them out (527), surely a parodistic allusion to Pater's dictum that "Venice is frozen music."

Gaddis continues this parody in his description of popular music. Running counter to Gibbs's quotation from Beethoven that "the better among us bear one another in mind" (290), the only music actually performed in the novel is, in effect, solipsistic, performed without anyone—or anything—in mind. The virtuoso referred to here is Rhoda's boyfriend, Al, the guitar player in a group Gaddis appropriately named the Gravestones. As the following passage indicates, the music they perform is indeed deadening, creating the same monotonous effect as the sound of the water that drips in incessant monotone from the entropic faucet in the Ninety-sixth Street flat:

> —No like go ahead I mean I'm for everybody doing what they want to man plunka, plunka plunk
> —look you don't understand I'm . . .
> —Like why not man I mean that's how it ought to be like everybody doing what they want to do, plunk plunk plunka . . . —like I mean what's that
> —what
> —Like that arrow you just made
> —What's this? It's a diminuendo don't you, you read music don't you? Plunk—like why do I want to read music man I mean I play music, like that's what music is isn't it man? I mean I play my own music what do I want to like read it for
> —Oh
> —Man like I play what I feel I mean not what some other cat writes for me to feel . . . plunk plunk plunk—like I mean I'm not one of your cats that has to sit down and play what some other cat hears I mean I make my own sound man . . . plunk. (551)

By describing the mindless and selfish monotone of both Al and his music in this manner, Gaddis creates an ironic counterpoint to the transforming power of the E-flat chord that goes on for 136 bars, reminding us that music can deaden as well as transform if we keep ourselves rather than one another in mind.

Rhoda manifests the same sort of egalitarian, ignorant, and reductive sensibility as her boyfriend. In looking over Gibbs's manuscript, she twice, in ironically revealing malapropisms, mispronounces the *agapē* portion of the book's title: once as agape and once as *pieta* (604–5). As Gibbs's response indicates, the ignorance that informs Rhoda's response is as deadening to the spiritual ideal of *agapē* as her boyfriend's performance is to the power of music: "Didn't Christ! didn't say pieta whole Goddamned different Christ any God damned use look, look don't bring a God damned thing to it can't take a God damned thing from it" (605). Craft and knowledge, uncharted territories for Rhoda and her boyfriend, must be actively brought to life, Gaddis is saying, and must be played with others in mind. Otherwise, the music of the world, a force that in the ways described above has the potential for overcoming the venal and mean-spirited world portrayed in this book, will be reduced to the Rhodas listening to their boyfriends' "plunka plunka plunka" with their minds and hearts agape rather than filled with *agapē*.

4 . . . . .

Carpenter's Gothic

The squirming facts exceed the squamous mind.
—*Wallace Stevens, "Connoisseur of Chaos"*

• • • In tracing the concept of the ethics of indeterminacy in Gaddis's novels, the collage of thought fragments assembled by the reader has included references within the text that, however oblique, help clarify the persistence of love: how some virtue of *agapē*, reflected in the thought of Rilke or Benjamin or Mozart, can endure and sustain itself in a world agape. In *Carpenter's Gothic*, however, Gaddis recasts the problem of ethics from how one might live deliberately in a world without absolutes to whether practicing the virtues of the ethics of indeterminacy in such a world is possible at all. In this novel there are plenty of people who live without absolutes, but their virtues of destabilization and corruption problematize rather than enhance the possibilities of love. Gaddis omits any reference to concepts such as "Dilige" or *agapē* in *Carpenter's Gothic*, instead relying on the symbolic resource of his previous work to provide a grisly reminder to anyone familiar with it of the mortal blow *agapē* suffers in this novel, a landscape that stands totally agape to the virtues of the ethics of indeterminacy.

Near the end of *The Recognitions* Stephen is comforting a bird that, startled, has flown into his hand. As he attempts to explain the ethical tenet of "Dilige et quod vis fac" to the novelist, Ludy, first by spelling it out in Latin and then translating it to "Love and do what you want to" (*R* 899), Stephen opens his hand and the bird flies away, a symbol of the freedom this love allows. Gaddis begins *Carpenter's Gothic* with another reference to a bird. Although there is initially some ambiguity concerning its species—"The bird, a pigeon, was it? or a dove" (1)—there is no ambiguity concerning its fate. Used as a baseball by some neighborhood kids, the bird is flung, hit, and caught, then hit again "into the yellow dead-end sign on the corner," Gaddis's chilling symbolic shorthand description of the fate love suffers (the reader finds out on page twenty-four that "it was a dove") in a world where almost no one gives voice to the concept of "Dilige" or anything like it.

Given the forceful excarnation of love in this novel, *Carpenter's Gothic* becomes a work that is at once easier and more difficult to embrace than either *The Recognitions* or *J R*. It is easier because the short length, easier-to-follow plot, and more conventional narrative style of *Carpenter's Gothic* depart markedly from the encyclopedic density and labyrinthine narrative form of the earlier works. It is more difficult, however, because despite its accessibility, the vision *Carpenter's Gothic* puts forth is decidedly bleak, and seems to deny any attempt the reader might make to transform it.

In *The Recognitions* and *J R* an important part of Gaddis's message is the need for hard work to extract any sort of meaning; reading novels, as Jack Gibbs reminds Edward Bast in *J R*, should be more difficult than going to the movies: "problem most God Damned readers rather be at the movies. Pay attention here bring something to it take something away problem most God damned writing's written for readers perfectly happy who they are rather be at the movies come in empty-handed go out the same way" (*J R* 289–90). If active engagement is the key to transforming noise to message in a cacophonous world, however, the question persists of just how many readers will struggle through 700 or 900 plus pages of difficult text. If, as J. D. O'Hara suggests, "Few Americans will be able or willing to read *J R*," then a novelist as concerned with morality and value as Gaddis appears to be must concern himself not only with making his vision illuminating but also with making it accessible.[1] Gaddis himself has commented on this issue, and the relative ease involved in summarizing *Carpenter's Gothic* does suggest that, having mapped out his major themes inside virtually impenetrable narrative jungles, Gaddis has decided to clear something of a path for the reader.[2]

Carpenter's Gothic certainly suggests a concern for accessibility not present in the earlier novels. For one thing, the conventions of fiction are scaled down to manageable proportions, what Gaddis has described as the "staples" of traditional narrative.[3] The setting of the novel is one house, and there are but five main characters: McCandless, the home's owner; Paul and Liz Booth, who rent the house; Liz's carefree brother, Billy; and the Reverend Elton Ude, much discussed although never actually present. Add to the novel's setting and characters a plot that although complex at least presents a cause/effect sequence, and what results is a sense of traditional narrative in which the author has resumed an active role in managing the text. This conventionality is further reinforced by the shape of discourse in *Carpenter's Gothic*. Although the novel uses unmediated dialogue, the small number of characters makes separating voices in this novel much easier than in *J R*. Even more significant are the numerous descriptive sections in *Carpenter's Gothic*, highly imagistic passages liberally sprinkled throughout the text that break up dialogue, providing an aesthetic distance from which the reader can more easily discern who is saying what to whom.

But if the formal and linguistic characteristics of *Carpenter's Gothic* present relatively few roadblocks to its readers, its content intractably resists those who would seek any emphatic, conventional affirmation of the theme present in Gaddis's earlier novels: humans' capacity, if they will but act on it, to transform through love an otherwise venal and mean-spirited world. Within the relatively simple landscape of *Carpenter's Gothic*, the reader who seeks out this theme quickly discerns an ethical pattern that perversely reformulates the truism that character is fate. Paul Booth, the character exposed as greedy and unfeeling, not only escapes punishment but prospers. A self-styled media consultant for the Reverend Elton Ude, Paul spends most of the novel creating tacky media events for his client while trying to escape imprisonment for being a bagman—one who passes the money in corporate bribes. Despite his bumbling nature, however, by the novel's end Paul has avoided jail and has inherited a fortune with which he can create further nefarious schemes. Paul's wife, Liz, the character who more than any other demonstrates a capacity for compassion and generosity, nevertheless contributes to Paul's schemes, including one that requires Liz to pay endless and humiliating visits to doctors to certify how injuries she suffered in an airline crash have caused Paul "conjugal distress." Unwilling to confront Paul, Liz confines expression of her integrity and sensitivity to the pages of her unfinished novel. When she finally does express moral outrage, it is against McCandless, and the indignation of her outburst is undercut by the malapropisms she uses to express it (Clausnitz for Clausewitz, Portuguese for Zambici) (241). The fatal heart attack she suffers at the end of the novel is suggestive: in a corrupt, greedy, and high-powered world, the well-intentioned heart bursts from pressure.

Or it gives in, an attitude demonstrated by the geologist McCandless. Despite his role as the indignant *vir bonus*, despite his constant ranting against the mindless excesses of government, religion, and society at large that impoverish the human spirit, McCandless literally sells out, accepting a sixteen thousand-

dollar payment from his former CIA crony, Lester, in exchange
for survey maps McCandless knows will help escalate military
tension in Africa (148, 246). Like Liz, McCandless cannot enact
his moral vision.

Any lingering doubt about the triumph of corruption is dis-
pelled by the sense of sleaze and Armageddon that ends *Carpenter's
Gothic*. The reader finds Paul, having just left Liz's funeral, trying
to seduce her best friend, Edie, by employing exactly the same
line he used at the funeral of Liz's father to romance Liz, that
he was "crazy about the back of your neck" (22, 262). Meanwhile,
the reader has just been told that a "10 K demo bomb" (259)
was detonated off the African coast, strongly suggesting that
McCandless's sellout and Paul's scheming have led the world to
the brink of World War III.

Of course, a bleak scenario is nothing new to Gaddis's fiction;
one would be hard pressed to describe what happens in either
The Recognitions or *J R* in more favorable terms. In those novels,
however, such bleakness is offset by the fact that the narrative
itself can be understood to function as an aesthetic mediating
presence, an artifact that teaches readers how to find their way
in a world without absolutes. If readers are willing to confront
these unstable narratives, they can restitch a raveled plot, uncover
an oblique allusion—in short, learn to recover meaning in life
by first learning how to recover it in fiction. For all their complexity and discontinuity, *The Recognitions* and *J R* are linguistic cathe-
drals, narratives replete with every manner of verbal quoin and
groin and pediment and lintel and rock-faced arch that, however
complex, can be used to construct a coherent and affirmative
narrative artifact by those readers willing to apprentice themselves
to Gaddis's vision.

Carpenter's Gothic, in contrast, does not offer the reader any
such means of using the text to offset the vision it portrays. In
a decidedly postmodern turn, this novel explicitly repudiates the

Utopian vision of such high modernists such as Le Corbusier and Frank Lloyd Wright to use architecture to transform social life. Like carpenter gothic, the architectural principle from which the novel derives its title, Carpenter's Gothic flatters only to deceive those who would seek any aesthetic solution through it. McCandless explains the principles as a "patchwork of conceits, borrowings, deceptions the insides a hodgepodge of good intentions like one last ridiculous effort at something worth doing" (228).[4] Despite the presence of fragmentary information in this novel, readers who seek to construct an aesthetic artifact are disappointed. When connections are made, when the fragments of narrative are sewn together, the tapestry is grim. If Carpenter's Gothic abandons aesthetic complexity to make its vision accessible, what it presents is a chilling suggestion, in form as well as content, that the attempt to redeem the greed and corruption of the commodity-driven postmodern Protestant ethic by finding something worth doing might well be a ridiculous effort.

Although it makes the novel easier to read, then, the accessibility of Carpenter's Gothic also places limits on how readers might use the novel to learn ways of affirming meaning in an indeterminate world. Because it does not contain the aesthetic complexities present in the earlier novels, Carpenter's Gothic does not lend itself to transformation into something that says to its readers, "Learn how to manage and transform the chaos and negativity within me so that you can learn to manage and transform the same discontinuity in the real world." Instead, this novel speaks to the reader of the limits of aesthetic mediation, enacting in narrative the fact that sometimes aesthetic, coherent solutions are simply not possible.

Like Gaddis's other novels, Carpenter's Gothic is a book that refers to other books and so refers to the processes of writing, reading, and interpretation. And, although there are certainly a number of references to literary and historical works (for example

Charlotte Brontë's *Jane Eyre* and C. M. Doughty's *Travels in Arabia Deserta*), the outside text that dominates *Carpenter's Gothic* is the Bible. Citations from both testaments serve as the touch-stone both for Reverend Ude's railings against secular humanism and for McCandless's scathing critiques of Fundamentalist dogma. Given this emphasis, plus Paul's malapropistic reference to "Ephu-sians"(203) and Billy's comment that "Paul was adopted so he was probably really a Jew" (225), a reader might conclude that the character Paul is an allusion to Paul of Tarsus. At the very least, Paul's actions serve as an ironic counterpoint to the message preached in Ephesians, especially the commands in chapter four "to cast aside corrupt communication," and in chapter six for the man to "so love his wife even as himself." More telling, however, is how much Gaddis's portrait of Paul is Nietzschean rather than orthodox, the power-hungry priest who for Nietzsche ravaged the teachings of Christ in the name of politics of priestly self-perpetuation. In *The Antichrist* Nietzsche establishes the problem of understanding Christianity as conflict between priest and phi-lologist. The former, exemplified by Paul and his "genius for lying," claims that the gospels are divinely inspired adequate signs so that, by selectively editing the sacred writings, he can enhance and consolidate power. In contrast, the philologist "sees *behind* the 'sacred books' . . . and cries 'swindle.' "[5] For Nietzsche, Christ's message is that all texts are inadequate signs to their subject: "Blessedness is not promised, it is not tied to any conditions: it is the only reality—the rest is a sign with which to speak of it."[6] The message of Christ is not in the word, in correct interpretation, but in the awareness that the kingdom of heaven is a condition of the heart in the present to which we can all have access by becoming as little children. Liz, age thirty-three (61) and one who bleats like a dove (163–64), thus can be seen as in a sense both Christ and the Holy Spirit, heartbreakingly brutalized by the bagman of the gospels.

Nietzsche understood that all priestly readings are fictions, and in a novel where the word *fiction* describes not only the failed or unfinished written texts of McCandless and Liz but also psychological ones described variously as "serviceable" (121), "lunatic," and "desperate" (157), personalized ("this fiction's all your own," 169), "shabby" (186), and "paranoid sentimental" (224), love also becomes a fiction.

Gaddis makes this clear through the deceptively simple technique of repetition, using the same description in different contexts to call into question the nature of love. On page 117, Liz, having overcome her Freudian fear of finding rattlesnakes in the mailbox, opens it to find a pornographic photo left there as a prank by some neighborhood boys (the dove killers?). Gaddis describes the scene as a "picture of a blonde bared to the margin, a full tumid penis squeezed stiff in her hand and pink as the tip of her tongue drawing the beading at its engorged head off in a fine thread." On page 162, Liz, now in bed with McCandless, enacts the scene she saw in the picture, "her fingertip tracing the vein engorged up that stiffening rise to the crown cleft fierce where the very tip of her tongue came to lead a glint of beading off caught in the sunlight." Then on page 257, Paul, stumbling upon Liz's diary/novel after her death, reads "her tongue tracing the delicate vein engorged up the stiffening rise to the head squeezed livid in her hand, drawing the beading off in a fine thread before she brought him in, surging to meet him for as long as it lasted." In a novel where "to remember what really happened . . . is the hardest thing" (169), the above scenes clarify the import of the refrain in the novel that "there's a very fine line between the truth and what really happens" (130, 136, 191, 193, 240).

By sandwiching the real event between two fictions, Gaddis problematizes the truth of love between Liz and McCandless. Liz, sensitive to the picture's reduction of intimacy to mere sex, crushes the picture and throws it in the trash, but is the picture of the two of them in bed any different? Throughout the middle scene with McCandless, Liz wants to talk, seeking the intimacy of communication so lacking in her life. For eleven pages (152–63) Gaddis lets readers eavesdrop on an extended pirouette of conflicting desires: female intimacy versus male intercourse. Throughout a fanciful discussion ranging in topics from traveling to Alpha Centauri to see through a telescope "what really happened" earlier in Liz's life to "babies, demanding to be born," McCandless presses himself both upon and on Liz only to have her come "up on that elbow again" (153, 157). By page 158 McCandless has had enough and, one leg in his trousers, starts to leave, drawn back only when Liz begins again her "intimate" probing that culminates on 162 with her enacting the event she earlier threw away. With the arrival of Liz's brother, Billy, the fact that their encounter is nothing more than sex becomes clear. McCandless, having found a new audience, no longer bothers to listen to Liz and even leaves, ignoring the plans he and Liz had just made to spend a romantic evening together in front of the fire. By the end of the book, Paul's discovery of the same scene in Liz's writing serves to remind readers of the comment Liz had made during the scene with McCandless about why people write: "I think people write because things don't come out the way they're supposed to be" (158). These parallel scenes problematize love: that which Liz discards in disgust becomes that which she clings to in experience becomes that which she clings to in memory becomes, discovered by someone else, the same masturbatory vignettte she discarded. Even more important, the intense self-reflexivity of these scenes shows readers that the very fine line beween the truth and what really happened lies beading on the page. The repetition of the same lines in different scenes keeps the reader trapped within the loop of the fiction of the text. There is no magic telescope available to see things as "they really happened" or romantic stories to make things "come out the way they're supposed to be"—just fictions of love feigning love into fictions.

Carpenter's Gothic extends this critique of love past the bedroom. The word *rift* describing Liz's body during the love-making on page 163 is also a reminder that the coming apocalypse is set in the Great Rift Valley in Kenya, a place where as a young man McCandless discovered fossils of the first human beings, the dawning of intelligence and of at least the possibility of love. Now, however, the significance of the rift is based on the fiction spread by the CIA that there is gold in the territory. The details are labyrinthian (McCandless spells out the scenario on pages 236–39), but the significance is clear. Hearkening back to *The Recognitions* (as well as to the sex scenes described above), McCandless tells Liz that there is no gold to forge: "The vein runs out" (239). Early in his career McCandless had discovered gold above the Limpopo in Africa, but for twenty years no one believed him (141). Now, Gaddis makes clear, the lack of "gold" as love or truth or intelligence doesn't matter: what does is the forging of fictions.

Gaddis further complicates any attempt to superimpose a recuperative interpretation by making the characters who succeed do so precisely because they reject the virtues of the ethics of indeterminacy. Lester and Paul certainly live deliberately in a world without absolutes, but their success results not from love but from the "deliberate cultivation of ignorance." McCandless uses this phrase to define the stupidity of simple-minded Fundamentalists (182), but the phrase also describes accurately the scenarios Lester fabricates to control the novel's political events. Like Paul, Lester is a Nietzschean "bad priest," a former Mormon missionary turned by the CIA. He recognizes that the truth is simply "anything to fill the emptiness any invention to make them part of some grand design anything the more absurd the better" (144). These are the fictions believed by those like Kinkead, the protagonist in McCandless's novel, who wants "to rescue his life from chance and deliver it to destiny" (137). The destiny of this world, however, is controlled by men such as Lester, who use whatever truth is appropriate to perpetuate what really happens. In *Carpenter's Gothic*, Marxist conspiracies and Fundamentalist revelations, like Kinkead's phrase, "to live deliberately" (139), have been reduced to fictions within fictions: naive expediencies in obscurantist scenarios designed to perpetuate destabilization, plunder, and death.

This is not to say, however, that *Carpenter's Gothic* does not stress the concern for understanding indeterminacy that informs Gaddis's earlier novels. Along with the restrictions it imposes on creating aesthetic coherence, the accessibility of *Carpenter's Gothic* also permits a freedom of understanding indeterminacy not allowed in either *The Recognitions* or *J R*. Despite its bleak interior, one should not ignore Gaddis's point, made several times in the novel, that the architecture of carpenter gothic (and *Carpenter's Gothic*) was meant to be seen from the outside. Rather than continue to show readers how to construct coherent meaning within an indeterminate text, as the earlier novels do, *Carpenter's Gothic* can be understood as a novel that makes readers look at the outside, makes them recognize how important it is not to try to turn indeterminacy into an a priori method. If for no other reason, the aesthetic complexity of the earlier novels stressed the role of reader as participant, one who learned by reading *The Recognitions* and especially *J R* those methods by which one could establish coherence within an indeterminate landscape. *Carpenter's Gothic*, in contrast, reminds readers that to methodize indeterminacy is to forget the reason for the concept: to describe a world in which all methods and testimonies risk being false. *Carpenter's Gothic*, in other words, does not invoke a collage of indeterminacy as a principle of composition capable of being transformed into order. Instead, it records indeterminacy as a subject meant to be comprehended phenomenalistically, without the accompaniment of an interpretative aesthetic pattern.

The narrative strategy that *Carpenter's Gothic* employs to insure that the reader recognizes the essential indeterminacy of the world involves the novel's use of facts, but facts used in a different way than in traditional realistic fiction. As Mas'ud Zavarzadeh points out in *The Mythopoeic Reality: The Post-Modern American Non-Fiction Novel*, traditional fiction used facts as elements of composition, as rhetorical devices that authenticate the particular concept expressed in the fiction.[7] Many characters and events in *Ulysses*, for example, have their counterpart in reality, but finally Joyce alters them for the purposes of authenticating the coherence of his particular vision. In *Carpenter's Gothic*, however, facts are not used to authenticate the verisimilitude of the author's vision. Instead, they are used as what Zavarzadeh describes in his analysis of nonfiction novels such as *In Cold Blood* as the transcription of facts as ends in themselves whose presence certifies the perplexity and ambiguity of the world that lies outside of fiction. By conferring equal status on fact and fiction, *Carpenter's Gothic* reminds readers that no matter how well they might manage a discontinuous text, there will always be the real world with which to contend, an indeterminate world in which, as Wallace Stevens reminds us, "the squirming facts exceed the squamous mind."

One such example of facts concerns the numerous references made to the tenets, beliefs, practices, and organizations of the evangelical Right. A cursory reading of *Carpenter's Gothic* might lead one to believe that the examples of revivalist piety and

reactionary populism are simply foils—authorially conceived—
against which a protagonist (McCandless) pushes a stock theme,
the evil consequences of supposedly divinely sanctioned stupidity.
The strategy appears straightforward: create characters and situations that demonstrate narrow-minded views, have another reasonable, cynical character expose these views as aberrations of
sound moral principles, and readers will have confirmed for them
once again the superiority of rational and humane values.

Throughout the novel, McCandless does just this, mercilessly
exposing how evangelicals are "doing business with the Bible,"
how they use literal interpretation of Scripture to reduce moral
complexities to a simple formulation: black versus white, us versus
them. As a former geologist and writer of science textbooks,
McCandless plays the role of a modern-day Clarence Darrow,
making mincemeat of biblical literalism with devil's-advocate
questions about puzzling, contradictory, and mean-spirited Fundamentalist applications of Scripture. Having been a participant in
a contemporary Scopes monkey trial played out in a town called
Smackover, Arkansas, as well has having been asked to write a
series of comic books designed to teach the "true" history of
creation unsullied by evolutionary theory, McCandless directs
much of his ridicule against creationism and censorship of texts.
The true target of McCandless's satire, however, is what he per-
ceives as revealed truth's most sinister consequence, "the deliberate cultivation of ignorance" (182): "Good God, talk about a
dark continent I'll tell you something revelation's the last refuge
ignorance finds from reason. Revealed truth is the one weapon
stupidity's got against intelligence and that's what the whole
damned thing is all about" (183). To support his assertion,
McCandless catalogs a series of excesses committed in the name
of revealed truth. Describing the trial in Smackover, McCandless
comments that

by defending the Bible against the powers of Darkness they're doing more to degrade it taking every damned word in it literally than any militant atheist could ever hope to. Foolishness bound in the heart of the child but the rod of correction shall drive it out so they whale the daylight out of their kids with sticks. And they shall take up serpents so they get liquored up and see how many rattlesnakes they can get into a burlap bag, talk about homo habilis in East Africa two million years ago. (134)

Shuffling through his papers, McCandless discovers a clipping about a Texas couple "who kept an eye out for school books that undermine patriotism, free enterprise, religion, parental author- ity, nothing official of course, just your good American vigilante spirit hunting down, where is it, books that erode absolute values by asking questions to which they offer no firm answers there, you see? Same damned thing, we've got the questions they've got the answers" (184). As McCandless points out, however, too often the nature of the answer is destructive. In a novel so concerned with structures, McCandless employs a suggestive metaphor in describing how evangelists "launder Genesis": "hand them Genesis and Revelation with a little of Jeremiah thrown in, the wormwood and gall and the Lord coming down like a whirlwind, is not my word like as a fire? saith the Lord; and like a hammer that breaketh the rock? Stupidity like that, you put a hammer in its hand and everything looks like a nail" (182). The consequences of such indiscriminate hammering in the name of God are what McCandless calls "the self-fulfilling prophecy" of apocalyptic revelation:

> The greatest source of anger is fear, the greatest source of hatred is anger and the greatest source of it all is this mindless revealed religion anywhere you look, Sikhs killing Hindus, Hindus killing Moslems,

Druse killing Maronites, Jews killing Arabs, Arabs killing Christians and Christians killing each other maybe that's the one hope we've got. You take the self-hatred generated by original sin turn it around on your neighbors and maybe you've got enough sects slaughtering each other from Londonderry to Chandligarh to wipe out the whole damned thing. (186)

Despite this scathing critique of revealed truth, however, the point of placing Fundamentalism in conflict with reason is not to claim reason's triumph but rather to expose just how fictional McCandless's humanistic premise is. Finally, the validity of his argument is compromised by his inability to act in accordance with it; because McCandless sells out, within this novel reason and humanistic values lose. Gaddis shows that the cynical diatribe McCandless makes against stupidity masks an even greater threat to humanism in general and agapistic ethics in particular, the loss of hope. It is no accident that in *Carpenter's Gothic* the expression "live deliberately" is spoken by Kinkead, the central character in McCandless's unfinished novel (139). The tenet central to *The Recognitions*, already parodied in *J R*, is now further reduced to the status of a hapless fiction written by a hapless man. A McCandless does not seek solutions by "living it through" or even by "bringing a god-damned thing to it." Instead, as Liz pointedly makes clear, McCandless ironically turns to prophecy as the final solution left to a sold-out bankrupt humanism—the prophecy of Armageddon: "You're the one who wants Apocalypse, Armageddon all the sun going out and the sea turned to blood you can't wait no, you're the one who can't wait! The brimstone and fire and your Rift like the day it really happened because they, because you despise their, not their stupidity no, their hopes because you haven't any, because you haven't any left" (244).

Of course, if the limitations or corruptibility of reason were confined simply to fiction characters and situations, a discerning reader would see this as only a qualified indictment. Although in practice humanism fails in this novel, in principle there could just as easily be a work in which a hero of reason and humanity triumphs over stupidity.

In *Carpenter's Gothic*, however, ignorance and stupidity are not simply rhetorical figures under the control of the author's imagination; they assume an extraliterary, factual dimension that cannot be circumscribed by aesthetic solutions. The Smackover monkey trial, for example, is not simply Gaddis's imaginative interpretation of evangelical theory; it is a recording, a transcription of an event that actually took place in December of 1981 in Arkansas.[8] The trial focused on the legality of Arkansas Act 590, a proposed law drawn up by the Institution for Creation Science. If enacted, the law would have required that the biblical account of Genesis would be the only theory of creation taught in Arkansas public schools. A similar transcription of extraliterary fact concerns the reference McCandless makes to a book-banning couple in Texas. This reference is not a mere fictional foil for McCandless's vision; it refers to Mel and Norma Gabler, cofounders of Education Research Analysts, a textbook-screening service operated out of their home in Longview, Texas (Longview is also the name Gaddis gives to the Booth family estate). The Gablers worked as a nationwide clearinghouse for textbooks, focusing their attention, like the "fictional" couple in *Carpenter's Gothic*, on the annual textbook adoption proceedings of the Texas Board of Education.[9] As Gaddis's novel corroborates, Texas is the nation's single largest purchaser of textbooks, and again as *Carpenter's Gothic* suggests, the Gablers, fictional and factual, did become influential enough that publishers began to modify texts along Fundamentalist Christian guidelines in anticipation of attacks by the Gablers and other groups. McCandless may call the fictional Gablers vigilantes or the townsfolk of Smackover (an actual place in southern Arkansas) "smug idiots with pious smiles" who "think God put them here in their cheap suits and bad neckties in his own image" (182), but *Carpenter's Gothic* finally tells its readers that more often than not it is as much the good folk of Smackover and the Gablers as it is people like McCandless who exist and prosper outside fictive boundaries.

Understood this way, the facts in *Carpenter's Gothic* are not used illustratively to unveil an aesthetic order amid chaos. Instead, the counterpoint of fact to fiction in this novel functions as a reminder of how much reality, in its unreasonable, unpredictable state, resists the coherence of rational humanism. *Carpenter's Gothic* in no way endorses the tenets of fundamentalist Christianity. However, the fact that the novel establishes the failure of reason and humanistic values (what Fundamentalists would call secular humanism) to tame the excesses of revealed truth also points to a rejection of conventional humanistic solutions.[10] Instead, the novel asks the reader to remember what its reference to V. S. Naipaul's *The Mimic Men* suggests, namely how fictive, how futile the quest for order can become in extreme situations: "I distrusted romance. See, though, how I yielded to it. A man, I suppose, fights only when he hopes, when he has a vision of order, when he feels strongly there is some connexion between the earth on which he walks and himself. But there was my vision of a disorder which it was beyond any one man to put right. There was my sense of wrongness, of beginning with the stillness of that morning of return" (150).[11]

In keeping with his demonstrated interest in morality, however, Gaddis does not allow such wrongness to be the only angle possible for a reader who looks at *Carpenter's Gothic* from the outside. If the counterpoint of fact and fiction reveals the inadequacy of humanism to redeem what Gaddis shows to be the latest incarnation of the inescapable Protestant ethic, it also provides the means with which the reader can, if not create, at least comprehend a third alternative to revealed truth and cynical humanism. It is ironic that the reader discovers an important clue to this third alternative by continuing to read Naipaul's negative novel. After relating the experience Gaddis cites, Ralph Kripsalsingh, *The Mimic Men*'s protagonist, goes on to "put things right" by finding within himself what Naipaul has elsewhere called the "slow magic of writing, the working toward unexpected conclusions."[12] Throughout most of *The Mimic Men*, Kripsalsingh is a writer in torment, seeking to discover coherence by writing his memoirs but instead only discovering how much language can distort and deceive. By the novel's end, however, Kripsalsingh comes to realize that in seeking to create coherence through writing, his gift of phrase was unreliable and destructive insofar as it emphasized concepts instead of the experience of actual events. Accordingly, he finds in language the power to record, to recreate actual events that he now sees as the necessary precondition for the establishment of any order. Only then can Kripsalsingh, with the acceptance of facts as the pivot of his memoirs, recognize what the right phrases are "to abolish that disturbance which is what a narrative in sequence might have led me to."[13] Once he is released from the pressure to impose coherence through language, the last few pages of *The Mimic Men* reveal that Kripsalsingh has, in his words, "cleared the decks, as it were, and prepared myself for fresh action. It will be the action of a free man."[14]

But how is the reader of *Carpenter's Gothic* to understand this freedom? If Naipaul finds purpose in the "slow magic of writing that leads to unexpected conclusions," where in Gaddis's novel, one in which aesthetics takes such a beating, is a linguistic third alternative clarified? Another clue is provided by several allusions to Robinson Jeffers's poem "Wise Men in Their Bad Hours," which remarks on the peculiar envy that intellectuals have for the sleepwalking masses "making merry like grasshoppers."[15] Such envy provides a counterpoint to the central idea of the poem—

that to have made "something more equal to the centuries / Than muscle and bone, is mostly to shed weakness." Understood in the context of *Carpenter's Gothic*, these lines take on more significance than a simple call to action, for how Jeffers would have his readers shed weakness can be understood as the third alternative to the humanist / evangelical conflict presented in Gaddis's novel.

Specifically, Jeffers's message was the need, as he put it in "The Inhumanist," "to break out of humanity, to shrug off their human God and their human godlessness / To endure this time."[16] Before it is possible to affirm life, Jeffers insists, humans must overcome their humanity, a slippery concept based on the premise that civilization's disease is humanity's love of self. Jeffers is arguing that man will not only have to abandon faith in his anthropomorphic God but will also, as Jeffers says in "Shine, Perishing Republic," "be in nothing so moderate as in love of man, a clever servant, insufferable master."[17] In this poem Jeffers portrays man's anthropomorphic tendencies as "the trap that catches noblest spirits," leading inevitably to "the thickening center; corruption," which in turn has led America, "in the mould of its vulgarity, heavily thickening to empire."[18] If there is value, the only true measuring stick is found outside of humans, among natural phenomena. But if to endure means to forgo humanity, what is left to affirm? For Jeffers, the answer was "to love the coast opposite humanity," to discard illusions about man and instead concentrate, as he puts it in "De Rerum Virtute," on nature itself: "One light is left us: the beauty of things, not men; / the immense beauty of the world, not the human world."[19] Jeffers deliberately avoided capitalizing the word *nature* to emphasize how his vision differed from the romantic worship of an oversoul. Instead of immanence of spirit, Jeffers focused on the separateness of the natural from the human as nature's most significant aspect, primarily because only through the recognition of the true existence of the not-human could humans ever hope to escape from egotism and despair, a recognition Jeffers describes in "Flight of Swans" as touching the "diamond within to the diamond outside":

> Sad sons of the stormy fall,
> No escape, you have to inflict and endure; surely it is time for you
> To learn to touch the diamond within to the diamond outside,
> Thinning your humanity a little between the invulnerable
> diamonds,
> Knowing that your angry choices and hopes and terrors are in
> vain,
> But life and death not in vain: and the world is like a flight of
> swans.[20]

Carpenter's Gothic, then, uses facts—narrative information whose existence is extratextual—not only to expose the existence of stupidity and the impotence of humanism but also to certify that a third alternative does exist with the potential for serving as a moral base without suffering the weaknesses inherent in more traditional humanism. But Carpenter's Gothic goes beyond simply acknowledging the existence of this other-directed perception espoused by Naipaul and Jeffers; the novel also gives readers a demonstration of how to use language to experience this nonhumanistic alternative.

As mentioned earlier, scattered throughout the dialogue of Carpenter's Gothic are examples of dense imagistic poetry whose apparent narrative function is to provide readers with a resting place from which they can better understand the dialogue. Read from another angle, however, the stress, enjambment, and rhythm of these passages point to the work of another poet who, like Jeffers, made the act of seeing and comprehending individual things apart from mankind a sine qua non for knowledge and moral responsibility—Gerard Manley Hopkins.

In what follows, lines typical of the descriptive passages in

Carpenter's Gothic, a reader can readily discern a "Hopkinesque" flavor to the prose. Describing a moment of Liz's melancholic life, Gaddis writes,

> From the terrace, where she came out minutes later, the sun still held the yellowing lights of the maple tree on the lower lawn's descent to a lattice fence threatening collapse under a summer exuberance of wild grape already gone a sodden yellow, brown spotted, green veined full as hands in its leaves' lower reaches toward the fruitless torment of a wild cherry tree, limbs like the scabrous barked trunk itself wrenched, twisted, dead where one of them sported wens the size of a man's head, cysts the size of a fist, a graceless Laocoon of a tree whose leaves where it showed them were shot through with bursts neither yellow nor not, whose branches were already careers for bittersweet just paling yellow, for the Virginia creepers in a vermillion haste to be gone. She looked up for the cry of a jay, for the sheer of its blue arc down the length of the fence and then back to lark bunting, red crossbill, northern shrike, lesser yellowlegs fluttering by on the pages of the bird book opened on her lap while here, in the branches of the mulberry tree above her, nothing moved but a squirrel's mindless leap for the roof of the house and she sat back, her stained face raised bared for the sun gone now even from the top of the maple, gone this abruptly behind the mountain with not even a cloud in what sky these leaves allowed to trace its loss leaving only a chill that trembled the length of her, sent her back in where she'd come from. (36)

If for no other reason than its focus on intense, natural imagery, this passage calls to mind "The Windhover" or "God's Grandeur." More significant, however, is how this and other descriptive passages in *Carpenter's Gothic* mirror Hopkins's techniques. Like Hopkins, Gaddis in this passage subordinates grammatical conventions to achieve what Hopkins called "sense-seizure," what one critic describes as Hopkins's "use of language to make the reader feel the experience being portrayed."[21] To help the reader reach the realm of experience through language, both writers, for example, freely convert verbs to nouns, string words together, and generally suspend (hyperbate) rather than clearly subordinate adjective / noun / verb qualifiers. The strongest evidence of shared concern with using form to affect meaning, however, is the degree to which both employ the gerund rather than the abstract word. As W. A. M. Peters points out, this idiosyncrasy was present in most of Hopkins's work, and the above passage clearly shows Gaddis's predilection for using this construction.[22]

And if the poetic form of this and other descriptive passages in *Carpenter's Gothic* mirrors that of Hopkins, it does so to generate the same effect that Hopkins sought: how language could bear witness to the inexhaustible "inscape" of things, Hopkins's term used to describe the outward reflection of the inner nature of the real.[23] Through this use of language, the reader is encouraged to see reality, to comprehend it by taking it in bits and pieces. To succeed at this, the reader must learn discrimination, the art of paying attention that for Hopkins has value per se: "All the world is full of inscape and chance left free to act falls into an order as well as a purpose: looking out my window I caught it in the random clods and broken heaps of snow made by the cast of a broom."[24]

Obliquely alluding to Hopkins and his style is not meant to provide readers with a means to assemble coherence, nor is it meant as a method for creating an affirmative aesthetic solution within the bleak landscape of *Carpenter's Gothic*. Instead, like the references to Fundamentalism already noted, the oblique allusions to Hopkins (like the more overt allusions to Jeffers and Naipaul) function as facts, transcriptions of real theories whose function in *Carpenter's Gothic* is to remind readers how they must act, believe, and use language to recover meaning outside of narrative interpretation in the real world. For Gaddis no less than for Hopkins, morality and value require not a dialogue between man and ideology, but one between eye and physical event. Gaddis seems to be saying in this novel that meaning does not disclose itself to reason, judgment, or rationalization. Instead, it is given in the very act of perception. In *The Recognitions* and *J R*, Gaddis in varying degrees refused to mediate for the reader. Nevertheless, if the reader were willing to work at it, the puzzles, the discontinuity of these texts could be transformed into meaningful structures. In *Carpenter's Gothic*, however, Gaddis takes his case for the essential contingency of meaning one step further. By writing an accessible narrative, by embedding fact and fiction in it, and by refusing to offer the reader a method by which the negative narrative can be aesthetically transformed, *Carpenter's Gothic* forces readers to look directly at the world's stupidity unmediated by any coherent aesthetic solutions. In response, one can, like McCandless, ineffectually and selfishly rave against the stupidity, or, like Hopkins, one can accept the importance of comprehending how the world is apart from the self.

Although in many ways more despairing of human possibility than either *The Recognitions* or *J R*, *Carpenter's Gothic* nevertheless offers a proposition of resolve, if not an aesthetic redemption. And, if the alternative of clear perception seems marginal compared with the chapter-and-verse transcription of stupidity and greed in *Carpenter's Gothic*, perhaps it is because we as readers ignore the point that Gaddis makes over and over again in his fiction: life is essentially problematic, and if we are to find anything worth doing in our lives it will not be through conceptualizing but through living. In the carpenter gothic society Gaddis portrays throughout his fiction, the ability to see clearly, to maintain a steadfast vision in the face of a hodgepodge of conceits is not marginal; it is the necessary precondition for allowing one, as Stephen / Wyatt Gwyon puts it in *The Recognitions*, "to live deliberately"; or as Jack Gibbs reminds us in *J R*, "to keep one another in mind."

The importance of enacting this vision cannot be overstated. As Gaddis reminds several times in *Carpenter's Gothic*, there is a "a very fine line between the truth and what really happens." The truth is still the moral code, the ideal of agapistic love that runs throughout Gaddis's narratives, but without being enacted it remains a hapless fiction, as the reduction of living deliberately to a statement made by a fictional character in McCandless's novel stresses. "What really happens" is what people do, whether motivated by compassion or by greed. And what happens most, Gaddis warns, is based on greed, is the ruthless combination of military spending and world markets whose only moral code is based on what improves performance and efficiency, even if it means endorsing terrorism. If, as Paul states, the "problem's just too many god-damned pieces" (212) for fiction to reconcile, then the reader is left to act on the hint provided by the omission of end punctuation in the novel's last sentence: assembling the "squirming facts," redeeming our inescapable Protestant ethic, has now become our responsibility.

. . . . .

Conclusion

Who then devised the torment? Love.
—*T. S. Eliot, "Little Gidding"*

• • • *The Recognitions, J R,* and *Carpenter's Gothic* are significant books—what I call epistemological novels—because they
recall origins and foresee endings, correlating the worlds of science, religion, art, and economics far more elaborately than
most other novels. More importantly, they can be considered
epistemological novels because they insist on the continuing responsibility of those who live in the present that lies between
such origins and endings. Through the peculiar indeterminacy
of their linguistic form, these novels dramatize the truth explained
by contemporary science. Readers of Gaddis come to realize what
Bohr and Heisenberg understood: life is not linear, aimed at
one fixed and beckoning point and seeking consummation there.
Structure is still important to understanding, but it is so adverbi-
ally, as a modifier of a more fundamental process of experience.
The truth of contemporary epistemology, whether in life or in
art that constitutes such truth narratively, requires ever-repeated
understandings in different contexts.

From the point of view of the detached, objective, Newtonian
observer, Gaddis's vision is bleak, a reminder of the shriveling
consequences imposed by the diminishing returns of humanity's

investment in structures that dissemble. If the outlook of the
detached observer is replaced by the insight of the involved reader,
however, what then emerges is the element otherwise obscured by
the books' visions of counterfeit, greed, and stupidity: humanity's
ability to confer meaning, however indeterminate or contingent.
In a narrow sense, those who criticize Gaddis are right: his difficult
prose and his carpenter gothic description of values offer readers
of these three novels no easy solutions. But Gaddis does make
us look at the world honestly through forms of language responsive
to the demands of contemporary explanations of truth, and that
is no small accomplishment. In so doing, Gaddis also reminds
the reader that true value, purpose, and meaning are not given
but contingent, products of responsible action that embrace the
essential indeterminacy of life. One can transform counterfeit,
can discover purpose amid the catastrophic ruins of past and
present failures and excesses.

But if moral action is, as Wyatt claims, "the only way we can
know ourselves to be real . . . the only way we can know others
are real" (R 591), the progression of Gaddis's work increasingly
makes it clear that we must risk acting on this knowledge, however
problematic the possibility for success. It is not simply for the
dark hilarity of the idea that Gaddis has, in a recent sketch,
reprised the character of J R, this time as a deputy assistant to
the Office of Management and Budget sent to testify about the
merit of the "trickle up" theory of federal government spending.[1]
Gaddis's forthcoming novel, A Frolic of His Own, explores the
vagaries of the law and the legal profession in a world where the
failure of a David Stockman simply means that he will be replaced
by a J R, more than ever a composite of opportunism and honesty
whose success Gaddis attributes "to obeying the letter of the law
and evading its spirit at every turn." J R's moral agenda is clear.
When questioned about the other problems of the economy, he
responds, "We'll burn those bridges when we come to them,

right?" To keep the connections in society intact, to avoid surrendering our world agape with no means to meaningfully traverse its paths, means making a juridical priority of linking our world with *agapē*. On page 155 of *Carpenter's Gothic* Gaddis describes McCandless's groping of Liz through a slight paraphrase of Eliot's lines in "East Coker," "as though to recover what had been lost and found and lost again and again," asking us to consider that to have an agapistic ethics, "the rest"—the groping, cupidity, and avarice of our world—cannot be "our business." For us, there is indeed "only the trying." However, to do so we must accept, as Hopkins reminds us, the juridical priority of choice:

> Man lives that list, that leaning of the will
> No wisdom can forecast by gauge or guess,
> The selfless self of self, most strange, most still,
> Fast furled and all foredrawn to No or Yes.[2]

Notes

Introduction

1. Bellah et al., *Habits of the Heart: Individualism and Commitment in American Life*, 3; MacIntyre, *After Virtue*, 8.
2. Lyotard, *The Postmodern Condition*, xxiii.
3. Gaddis, *J R*, 237, hereafter cited in the text. Gaddis's other novels are *The Recognitions*, hereafter cited in the text, abbreviated *R* when necessary, and *Carpenter's Gothic*, hereafter cited in the text, abbreviated *C's G* when necessary.
4. Bersani, *The Culture of Redemption*.
5. Instructive glosses on this controversial topic include Hassan, *The Post-Modern Turn*; Jencks, *What Is Postmodernism?*; and McCaffery, ed., *Postmodern Fiction*.
6. In a letter to me dated April 8, 1993, Steven Moore recounts that "Gaddis told me he heard a fellow student at Harvard use this line and he never forgot it. He didn't know if the student was quoting something or whether it was his own formulation."
7. Abadi-Nagy, "The Art of Fiction CI: William Gaddis," 77.
8. *The Writings of Henry David Thoreau*, vol. 2, *Walden*, 123. Hereafter cited in text.
9. Generally speaking, criticism of Gaddis tends to fall into two categories: identification of sources and discussion of themes in isolation. Typical of the first category is Koenig's "Recognizing Gaddis's *Recognitions*," which includes extensive quotations from Gaddis's manuscripts. Arguably the most enlightening examination of source material for *The Recognitions* is Leverence's article, "Gaddis Anagnoresis," which examines the influence of alchemy while adding vital information concerning Gaddis's baroque prose style. Weisenberger's "Contra Naturam?" analyzes source material for *J R*, specifically the influence of Wagner and Empedocles. Salemi's article, "To Soar in

Atonement," is a most complete examination of themes in this novel, while Le Clair, in "William Gaddis, *J R*, and the Art of Excess," and Theilemans's "Gaddis and the Novel of Entropy," have explained how the themes of excess and entropy inform *J R*. Theilemans also published the first essay-length study on *Carpenter's Gothic*, "Intricacies of Plot: Some Preliminary Remarks to William Gaddis's *Carpenter's Gothic*." Dewey also devotes a section to *Carpenter's Gothic* in *In a Dark Time*, 190–205. Two good collections containing interviews, essays, and bibliographies on Gaddis exist: a special issue of the *Review of Contemporary Fiction* 2, no. 2 (Summer 1982), and Kuehl and Moore, eds., *In Recognition of William Gaddis*. Moore has written two books on Gaddis, *A Reader's Guide to William Gaddis's "The Recognitions"* and *William Gaddis*.

10. Leverence's "Gaddis Anagnoresis," Moore's *William Gaddis*, mentioned above, and Le Clair's *The Act of Excess* are exempt from this judgment in their insightful examination of how form might reflect content in Gaddis's work.

11. Johnston, *Carnival of Repetition*, 3. LaCapra also applies Bakhtin's theories to Gaddis in "Singed Phoenix and the Gift of Tongues."

12. Although Johnston does not discuss the issue, the relationship between ethics and literature is important to Bakhtin, as Patterson discusses in *Literature and Spirit*.

13. Klinkowitz, *Literary Disruptions*, 32.

14. Chambers, *Thomas Pynchon*, 3.

15. Pynchon, *V.*, *a novel*, 366; Pynchon, *Gravity's Rainbow*.

16. Chambers, *Thomas Pynchon*, 3.

17. Derrida, *Writing and Difference*, 296.

18. Benjamin, "On the Mimetic Faculty," in *Reflections*, 336.

19. Benjamin, *The Origin of German Tragic Drama*, 184.

20. Benjamin, "One Way Street" and Other Writings, 62.

21. Jennings discusses this concept of reading on pp. 117–18 of *Dialectical Images*.

22. McHoul, "Labyrinths" (the notion of the postethical is further extended by McHoul and Wills in *Writing Pynchon*); Wilde, *Horizons of Assent*.

23. Wilde, *Horizons of Assent*, 10. Wilde's position remains essentially unchanged in his most recent work, *Middle Grounds: Studies in Contemporary American Fiction*.

24. McHoul, "Labyrinths," 211.
25. See the essays by Miriam Fuchs, "Il miglior fabbro': Gaddis' Debt to T. S. Eliot" and Koenig, "The Writing of *The Recognitions*," both in Kuehl and Moore, ed., *In Recognition of William Gaddis*. Koenig points out that at one point in the composing of *The Recognitions* Gaddis had intended to incorporate every line of the *Four Quartets* into the novel.
26. For a thorough discussion of Broch's concept of *Dichtung*, see Schlant, *Hermann Broch*.
27. Broch, *Breife von 1929 bis 1951*, 23.
28. Broch, *The Sleepwalkers*. This point is made in chapter 9 of the essay contained within the novel, entitled "Disintegration of Values," 561.
29. Broch, "Joyce and the Present Age," 89. For an explanation of Broch's concern with ethics rendered through experimental narrative, see Ziolkowski, "Hermann Broch and Relativity in Fiction"; Schlant, "Hermann Broch and Modern Physics."
30. Jameson, foreword to *The Postmodern Condition*, 19; Eco, *Travels in Hyper Reality*, 135–44.
31. Caputo, *Radical Hermeneutics*. A discussion of this concept appears in chapter 8.
32. Moore has been the Boswell (and much more) to Gaddis's Johnson. His pioneering, incisive work and steadfast support of other Gaddis scholars are in large part what has rescued Gaddis from critical obscurity. Moore's three books on Gaddis, cited in note 10, are highly recommended.

Chapter 1

1. Rorty, *Consequences of Pragmatism*, 163.
2. Lovin and Reynolds, eds., *Cosmogony and Ethical Order*, 8.
3. Toulmin, *The Return to Cosmology*, 53.
4. Quoted in Brans, *Listen to the Voices*, 171.
5. Quoted in Kuhn, *The Structure of Scientific Revolutions*, 44.
6. Rawls, *A Theory of Justice*.
7. MacIntyre, *After Virtue*. On page 208, he writes, "Narrative history of a certain kind turns out to be the basic and essential genre for the characterization of human action."

8. For a representative study of how contemporary philosophy considers issues of epistemology, see Duran's "Reliabilism, Foundationalism, and Naturalized Epistemic Justification Theory."
9. A recent example is Susan Strehle's *Fiction in the Quantum Universe.* This book's otherwise insightful readings of several postmodern novelists are marred by a lack of evidence clearly connecting the narratives discussed to quantum theory.
10. For Newton's thoughts on this subject, see Manuel, *Portrait of Isaac Newton.*
11. Barrow, *Theories of Everything,* 11.
12. Ibid., 210.
13. For a lucid discussion of this slippery subject, see Bremermann, "Complexity and Transcomputability."
14. Gödel, *On Formally Undecidable Propositions,* 7. For a discussion of the implications of Gödel's proof, see also Nagel and Newman, *Gödel's Proof.*
15. Barrow *Theories of Everything,* 32–33, discusses this topic.
16. For a complete discussion of this point, see Jauch, *Are Quanta Real?* A strong, perhaps radical, argument for the direct influence of quantum laws on living organisms at all levels of complexity is that of Jordan, *Physics of the Twentieth Century,* 150ff.
17. For a discussion of the genesis of this theory, see d'Abro, *The Rise of the New Physics,* 2:948–49.
18. Bohr's concept was apparently first annunciated in a 1927 article, "The Quantum Postulate and the Recent Development of Atomic Theory," reprinted in his *Atomic Theory and the Description of Nature,* 52ff.
19. Rorty elaborates on this distinction in *Philosophy and the Mirror of Nature.*
20. Many noted physicists have discussed this issue. See, for example, Bohr, *Atomic Physics and Everyday Life;* Born, *The Restless Universe;* Planck, *The Philosophy of Physics;* Heisenberg, *Across the Frontiers;* Bohm, *Causality and Chance in Modern Physics.* An excellent overview of the aesthetic nature of contemporary science is Weschler, ed., *On Aesthetics in Science.*
21. Quoted in Matson, *The Broken Image,* 131. Representative of the "sober" scientific objection to Oppenheimer's analogy is physicist Laurence Rosenhein's "Letter to Richard Pearce in Response to

'Pynchon's Endings.' " For an excellent discussion of how some quantum physicists continue to quest unsuccessfully for a unified theory, see Weinberg, *Dreams of a Final Theory*.

22. Kristeva, *Essays in Semiotics*; Derrida, *Of Grammatology*.

23. For a discussion of the controversy surrounding the Einstein, Podolsky, and Rosen (EPR) thought experiment designed to refute the attack on causality made by quantum mechanics, see David Park, *The How and the Why*, 341–44.

24. Misner et al., *Gravitation*, 1273.

25. Sartre, *Existentialism*, 27.

26. For a general introduction to the concept of *agapē*, see Nygren, *Agapē and Eros*; Fletcher, *Situation Ethics: The New Morality*; Outka, *Agapē*.

27. Davidson, *Inquiries into Truth and Interpretation*, 192.

28. Murdoch, "The Sublime and the Good," 51.

29. Caputo, *The Mystical Element in Heidegger's Thought*, 118–27, 173–83; Caputo, *Radical Hermeneutics*, 267.

30. Caputo, *Radical Hermeneutics*, 212.

31. For a fruitful discussion of second-order ethics, see Ross, *The Right and the Good*.

32. Niebuhr, *An Interpretation of Christian Ethics*, 73.

33. Quoted in Brown, *Life Against Death*, 141.

34. Smith, "When Love Becomes Excarnate," 106.

35. Abadi-Nagy, "The Art of Fiction CI," 61. In this interview Gaddis observed, "I tried to make it clear that Wyatt was the very height of a *talent* but not a genius—quite a different thing."

36. Gaddis's comment on the character J R appears in Miriam Berkeley's "PW Interviews: William Gaddis," 57.

37. Nietzsche's commentary on *ressentiment* can be found throughout *On the Genealogy of Morals* (1887). Danto presents a clear discussion of *ressentiment* in "Some Remarks on *The Genealogy of Morals*."

38. Steven Moore comments that *Redemption's* "Russian title, *Zhivoi trup* (1900), is properly translated *The Living Corpse*. *Redemption* is the title Arthur Hopkins used when first producing the play in New York (1918); Gaddis's use of the latter title stresses the importance of redemption in his novel" (*A Reader's Guide to William Gaddis's "The Recognitions,"* 241).

39. The statement about "doing" or "having business with the Bible"

runs throughout *Carpenter's Gothic*. The quotation from Nietzsche appears in *The Antichrist*, 45.

40. From Schiller's *Jungfrau von Orleans*. The quotation appears in the text of *J R* in German: "Mit der Dummheit kampfen Gotter selbst vergebens."

41. Abadi-Nagy, "The Art of Fiction CI," 79.

42. Stout, *Ethics after Babel*, 74–77; Minson, *Genealogies of Morals*, 3.

43. Abadi-Nagy, "The Art of Fiction CI," 61.

44. By competence I mean something different from the idea of literary competence put forth by Stanley Fish. Because Gaddis presents specific (if oblique) instructions to his readers, the problem of intuitive knowledge as the source of authority conceded by Fish is avoided.

45. Derrida, *Of Grammatology*, 139–40.

46. Barthes, "Style and its Image," 6–7.

47. Hayles, *The Cosmic Web*; Nadeau, *Reading from the New Book on Nature*.

48. Hayles, *The Cosmic Web*, 197; Nadeau, *Readings from the New Book on Nature*, 194.

49. Heidegger, *Identity and Difference*, 73.

50. Heisenberg, *Physics and Philosophy*, 174.

51. Peterson, "The Philosophy of Neils Bohr," 16.

52. For a detailed discussion of this concept, see Miller, *Imagery in Scientific Thought*, 155ff.

53. Quoted in Clifford Hooker, "The Nature of Mechanical Reality: Einstein versus Bohr," in Colodny, ed., *Problems and Paradoxes*, 139.

54. Group Mu, ed., *Collages*.

55. Benjamin, "The Artist as Producer," 98.

56. Frisby, *Fragments of Modernity*, 211–12.

57. Benjamin, *Illuminations*, 39.

58. Frisby, *Fragments of Modernity*, 188.

59. Benjamin, *Illuminations*, 37.

60. Frisby, *Fragments of Modernity*, 214.

61. Jennings, *Dialectical Images*, 178–82.

62. Benjamin, "On the Mimetic Faculty," in *Reflections*, 336.

63. Frisby, *Fragments of Modernity*, 189.

64. This concept is discussed in Culler, *The Pursuit of Signs*, 103–4.

65. Chasing allusions is always tricky business; see, for example, Bernard Benstock's howler linking Joyce to Gaddis, which is discussed in Moore's *William Gaddis*, 6–7. Still, Gaddis requires readers to take chances, and the parallels between Gaddis and Benjamin do not seem to exceed the limits set both by evidence and by common sense.

Chapter Two

1. See Peter (*aka* David) Koenig's " 'Splinters from the Yew Tree': A Critical Study of William Gaddis's *The Recognitions*" (Ph.D. diss., New York University, 1971). Koenig's study benefits from direct access to Gaddis's manuscripts and notes. Steven Moore was the first person to note Gaddis's use of Jung. (See note 6 below.)
2. Eliot, "Ulysses, Order, and Myth," 270.
3. Frazer, trans., *Apollodorus, the Library*, xxvii.
4. See Jung, *The Symbolic Life*, 18:748–50.
5. Spengler, *The Decline of the West*, 97–114.
6. On page 23, note 15, of *A Reader's Guide to William Gaddis's "The Recognitions,"* Steven Moore comments that Jung's first book-length study of alchemy, *The Integration of the Personality*, served as Gaddis's main source for the alchemical references in *The Recognitions*. Jung's book was later revised and expanded as *Psychology and Alchemy* (*Collected Works*, vol. 12).
7. For an overview of exoteric and esoteric alchemy, see Fabricius, *The Medieval Alchemists and their Royal Art*.
8. Besides Jung, the most thorough analysis of the philosophical aspects of esoteric alchemy is Gray's *Goethe the Alchemist*.
9. Cunnar, "Donne's 'Valediction: Forbidding Mourning,' " 83.
10. Ibid., 77.
11. Koenig, " 'Splinters from the Yew Tree,' " 90.
12. Jung, *Psychology and Alchemy*, 260.
13. See, for example, Harnack, *Outlines of the History of Dogma*.
14. Jung, *Psychology and Alchemy*, 23.
15. Ibid., 306.
16. Edwards, "Fermat's Last Theorem."
17. Gaddis explains the central role of alchemy in his notes: "First there is the ideal. Then the crash of reality; and chaos and death. Then

resurrection, in which the two working together, achieve redemption. Wyatt *is* the alchemist; there's no nearer parallel." Quoted by Koenig, " 'Splinters from the Yew Tree,' " 87.

18. Moore makes this observation on page 21 of *A Reader's Guide to William Gaddis's "The Recognitions."* Majer's statement is found in Jung, *Psychology and Alchemy*, 431.

19. Goody and Watt, "The Consequences of Literacy," 57.

20. Ibid., 57–58.

21. Graves, *The White Goddess*, 479.

22. Jonas, *The Gnostic Religion*, 37.

23. Arthur, *The Wisdom Goddess*, 14.

24. Moore, "Chronological Difficulties in the Novels of William Gaddis."

25. Koenig, for example, argues this point several times.

26. Leverence, "Gaddis Anagnoresis."

27. Croll, "The Baroque Style in Prose."

28. Ibid., 104.

29. Ibid., 112.

30. This assumption is not totally frivolous. Commenting on the writing of *The Recognitions* in his *Publisher's Weekly* interview, Gaddis offered the following: "I thought, 'I've got to get it all in here.' It's like that story of Tolstoy—I don't know if it's true—after he'd finished *War and Peace* and it was off at the printer's. He woke up striking his forehead and said, 'My God! I left out the yacht race!' " (Berkeley, "PW Interviews," 57).

31. See, for example, Kermode, *The Genesis of Secrecy*; Robert C. Tannehill, *The Sword of His Mouth* (Philadelphia: Fortress Press, 1975); Funk, *Jesus as Precursor*. Gaddis, an acknowledged admirer of Tolstoy (see preceding note), is no doubt familiar with Tolstoy's claim in *What Is Art* that parable is the highest form of literary expression.

32. Rilke, *Duino Elegies*, trans. Leishman and Spender, 9.

33. Ibid.

34. Rilke, *Duino Elegies*, trans. Young, 10.

35. Peters, *R. M. Rilke*, 185.

36. Rilke, *Duino Elegies*, trans. Garmey and Wilson, 102.

37. Rilke, *Duino Elegies*, trans. Leishman and Spender, 77.

38. Hartman, *The Unmediated Vision*, 98.

39. Peters, R. M. Rilke, 148.
40. Hartman, The Unmediated Vision, 168.
41. Purtscher, Rilke, Man and Poet, 197.
42. Rilke, Duino Elegies, trans. Young, 99.
43. Ibid., 92.
44. Rilke, Sonnets to Orpheus, 93.

Chapter Three

1. Fullerton, "Calvinism and Capitalism."
2. Ibid., 166.
3. Frederic Jameson, Introduction to Lyotard, The Postmodern Condition, xiii.
4. Baudrillard, "The Ecstasy of Communication," 127, 131.
5. Mandel, Late Capitalism. For a fuller discussion of this issue see Jameson, Postmodernism, or, the Cultural Logic of Late Capitalism. Maltby presents a different interpretation of Mandel in Dissident Postmodernists, 12–13.
6. The phrase "what's worth doing" appears numerous times in the text, uttered by a variety of characters.
7. Eco, The Open Work; Derrida, Spurs, 107.
8. Steiner, "Books: Crossed Lines."
9. Benjamin, Illuminations, 180.
10. I am indebted to James L. Rolleston for clarifying Benjamin's dialectical and often complex definition of art. For an in-depth discussion of this subject, see his "The Politics of Quotation."
11. Frisby, Fragments of Modernity, 226.
12. Benjamin, Charles Baudelaire, 103.
13. See, for example, Braudel, Capitalism and Material Life, 1400–1800.
14. For an assessment of the attacks against the institution of paper money, see Parrington, Main Currents in American Thought, 532–41.
15. For a relevant discussion, see Shell, The Economy of Literature.
16. Quoted in Rather, The Ring of Self-Destruction, 135.
17. Ibid., 135–36. Steven Moore disputes the significance I ascribe to the word rustling, pointing out that Ernest Newman offers a different translation in Wagner as Man and Artist. Although it is clear that Gaddis does rely on Newman for much of the Wagneria in J R,

Gaddis also expressed, in a letter to the author dated September 29, 1987, his pleasure in my "further explication of the prolonged E-flat opening [of] Das Rheingold." Hence, the interpretation offered here stands.

18. Rather, *The Ring of Self-Destruction*, 175.
19. Ibid., 161.
20. Ibid., 162.
21. For an excellent discussion of information theory, especially its relationship to the arts, see Moles, *Information Theory and Esthetic Perception*.
22. Malmgren, *Fictional Space in the Modernist and Post-Modernist American Novel*, 118.
23. Fries, *The Structure of English*.
24. Ibid., 294.
25. Benjamin, "The Work of Art in the Age of Mechanical Reproduction," in *Illuminations*, 219–53; Benjamin, "The Destructive Character" in *Reflections*, 301–3.
26. Norris, "Image and Parable," 17.
27. Frisby, *Fragments of Modernity*, 231.
28. Benjamin's distinction between the aestheticizing of politics and the politicizing of aesthetics runs throughout "The Work of Art in the Age of Mechanical Reproduction."
29. Roberts, *Walter Benjamin*, 200.
30. Benjamin, "Theses on the Philosophy of History," in *Illuminations*, 255-66; 264.
31. Broch, *The Sleepwalkers*, 648.
32. See, for example, Wheeler, *Josiah Willard Gibbs*. For Adams's misinterpretation of Gibbs, see Samuels, *Henry Adams*, 440–48.
33. Wheeler, *Josiah Willard Gibbs*, 81.
34. Jaynes, "Gibbs versus Boltzmann Entropies."
35. Wiener, *The Human Use of Human Beings*. For further discussion on why it is incorrect to interpret entropy only as a metaphor of destruction and chaos, see Kubat and Zeman, eds., *Entropy and Information in Science and Philosophy*, 350ff; Brush, "Thermodynamics and History"; Holton, "Presupposition in the Construction of Theories."
36. Wiener, *The Human Use of Human Beings*, 35.
37. Halio, "American Dreams," 840.

38. Einstein, *Mozart*, 465.
39. For Mozart's understanding of *agapē*, see Chailly, *The Magic Flute*, esp. "Cosmogony of Libretto," 92–97.
40. Rather, *The Ring of Self-Destruction*, 104.
41. Ibid., 139–42.
42. Prier, *Archaic Logic*, 145. One is also tempted to apply the cosmology of C. S. Peirce to this aspect of the novel, given Peirce's notion of evolutionary ethics progressing from tychism (chance) through fallibism to agapism.
43. For an excellent overview of the history of dialogue, see Ong, *Ramus*.
44. Quoted in Turkle, *Psychoanalytic Politics*, 86.
45. Nietzsche, *The Birth of Tragedy*, 102–3, 145–49.
46. Bakhtin, *The Dialogic Imagination*, 27.
47. Malmgren, *Fictional Space in the Modernist and Post-Modernist American Novel*, 117.

Chapter Four

1. O'Hara, "Boardwalk and Park Place versus Chance and Peace of Mind," 523–26.
2. See, for example, Grove, "Harnessing the Power of Babble."
3. Ibid., B10.
4. For a visual introduction to this style of architecture, see Maass, *The Gingerbread Age*, esp. chap. 3, "American Gothic." A more speculative discussion on the relationship between carpenter gothic architecture and the emotive fundamentalism presented in Gaddis's novel can be found in Early, *Romanticism and American Architecture*, esp. chap. 4, "The Gothic as a Style for Protestantism."
5. Nietzsche, *The Antichrist*, 47.
6. Ibid., 33.
7. Zavarzadeh, *The Mythopoeic Reality*, esp. chap. 1.
8. For a summary of this trial, see Flake, *Redemptorama*, 39–40.
9. Ibid., 42.
10. Gaddis underscores this failure by using the surname "Booth," quite possibly an ironic allusion to William and Katherine Booth, cofounders of the Salvation Army, avowed humanists, and strong critics

of "doing business with the Bible." In *Carpenter's Gothic*, of course, Paul Booth actively supports Ude's Fundamentalist business.

11. Gaddis acknowledges the quotation on the title page of *Carpenter's Gothic*.
12. White, *V. S. Naipaul*, 178.
13. Ibid., 179.
14. Naipaul, *The Mimic Men*, 300.
15. The source of these lines is also acknowledged by Gaddis on the title page of *Carpenter's Gothic*.
16. Jeffers, "The Inhumanist," in *The Double Axe and Other Poems*, 113.
17. Jeffers, "Shine, Perishing Republic," in *The Selected Poetry of Robinson Jeffers*, 168.
18. I am indebted to Steven Moore for clarifying for me the significance of this poem to Gaddis: "Gaddis read (['Shine, Perishing Republic'] out loud when I visited him in 1984, & he was thinking of working in some of its lines into *C's G*, even using one of its phrases—'thickening to empire'—as a possible title" (letter to author, August 28, 1987). See Moore's comment in *William Gaddis*, 151, explanation to note 10.
19. Jeffers, "De Rerum Virtute," in *Hungerfield and Other Poems*, 93.
20. Jeffers, "Flight of Swans," in *The Selected Poetry of Robinson Jeffers*, 577.
21. Weiss, ed., *Selections from the Notebooks of G. M. Hopkins*, 16.
22. Peters, *Gerard Manley Hopkins*, 135.
23. Hopkins himself never specifically defined *inscape*. For a valiant attempt to clarify this subject, see ibid., chapter one.
24. Hartman, *The Unmediated Vision*, 159. For a discussion that focuses on the linguistic rather than the theological basis of Hopkins's metaphysics, see Motto, " 'Mined with a Motion' "; Milroy, *The Language of Gerard Manley Hopkins*.

Conclusion

1. Gaddis, "Trickle-Up Economics."
2. Hopkins, "On the Portrait of Two Beautiful Young People," in *Poems of Gerard Manley Hopkins*, 170.

Bibliography

Abadi-Nagy, Zoltan. "The Art of Fiction CI: William Gaddis." *Paris Review* 105 (Winter 1987):54–89.

Abbas, Ackbar. "On Fascination: Walter Benjamin's Images." *New German Critique* 16 (1989):43–62.

Arnheim, Rudolph. *Entropy and Art: An Essay on Order and Disorder.* Berkeley: University of California Press, 1971.

Arthur, Rose. *The Wisdom Goddess: Feminine Motifs in Eight Nag Hammadi Documents.* Lanham, Md.: University Press of America, 1984.

Bakhtin, Mikhail. *The Dialogic Imagination.* Translated by Caryl Emerson and Michael Holquist. Austin: University of Texas Press, 1981.

Barrow, John. *Theories of Everything: The Quest for Ultimate Explanation.* Oxford: Clarendon Press, 1991.

Barth, John. "The Literature of Exhaustion." *Atlantic Monthly* 238 (August 1976): 31–40.

———. "The Literature of Replenishment." *Atlantic Monthly* 245 (January 1980): 67–72.

Barthes, Roland. *Music-Image-Text.* Translated by Stephen Heath. New York: Hill and Wang, 1977.

———. "Style and Its Image." In *Literary Style: A Symposium*, edited by Seymour Chatman. London and New York: Oxford University Press, 1971. 2–9.

Baudrillard, Jean. "The Ecstasy of Communication." In *The Anti-Aesthetic: Essays on Postmodern Culture*, edited by Hal Foster. Seattle: Bay Press, 1983.

Becker, Carl. *The Heavenly City of the Eighteenth-Century Philosophers.* New Haven: Yale University Press, 1959.

Bellah, Robert, et al. *Habits of the Heart: Individualism and Commitment in American Life.* Berkeley and Los Angeles: University of California Press, 1985.

Benjamin, Walter. *Charles Baudelaire: A Lyric Poet in the Era of High Capitalism.* Translated by Harry Zohn. London: Fontana, 1973.

———. *Illuminations.* Translated by Harry Zohn. London: Fontana, 1973.

———. *"One Way Street" and Other Writings.* Translated by E. Jephcott and K. Shorter. London: New Left Books, 1979.

———. *Reflections.* Translated and edited by Peter Demetz. New York: Schocken Books, 1986.

———. *The Origins of German Tragic Drama.* Translated by George Osborne. London: New Left Books, 1977.

———. *Understanding Brecht.* Translated by Anna Bostock. London: New Left Books, 1977.

Benstock, Bernard. "On William Gaddis: In Recognition of James Joyce." *Wisconsin Studies in Contemporary Literature* 6 (1965): 177–89.

Berkeley, Miriam. "PW Inteviews: William Gaddis." *Publishers Weekly,* July 12, 1985, 56–57.

Bersani, Leo. *The Culture of Redemption.* Cambridge: Harvard University Press, 1990.

Bohm, David. *Causality and Chance in Modern Physics.* Philadelphia: University of Pennsylvania Press, 1957.

Bohr, Niels. *Atomic Physics and Everyday Life.* New York: Wiley Press, 1958.

———. *Atomic Theory and the Description of Nature.* Cambridge: Cambridge University Press, 1934.

Booth, Wayne. *A Rhetoric of Irony.* Chicago: University of Chicago Press, 1974.

Born, Max. *The Restless Universe.* New York: Dover Publications, 1957.

Brans, Jo. *Listen to the Voices: Conversations with Contemporary Writers.* Dallas: Southern Methodist University Press, 1988.

Braudel, Fernand. *Capitalism and Material Life, 1400–1800.* Translated by Miriam Kochen. New York: Harper and Row, 1975.

Bremermann, Hans J. "Complexity and Transcomputability." In *The Encyclopedia of Ignorance,* edited by Ronald Duncan and Miranda Weston-Smith, 167–74. Oxford: Pergamon Press, 1977.

Broch, Hermann. *Breife von 1929 bis 1951.* Edited by Robert Pick. Zurich: Rhein, 1957.

Bibliography

———. "Joyce and the Present Age." In *A James Joyce Yearbook*, edited by Maria Jolas, 49–70. Paris: Transition Press, 1949.

———. *The Sleepwalkers*. Translated by Willa and Edwin Muir. San Francisco: North Point Press, 1985.

Brown, Norman O. *Life Against Death: The Psychoanalytical Meaning of History*. Middletown, Conn.: Wesleyan University Press, 1959.

Brush, Stephen. "Thermodynamics and History." *Graduate Journal* 7 (1967): 477–566.

Burtt, E. A. *The Metaphysical Foundations of Modern Science*. Garden City, N.Y.: Doubleday Anchor Books, 1955.

Caputo, John. *The Mystical Element in Heidegger's Thought*. Athens: Ohio University Press, 1978.

———. *Radical Hermeneutics: Repetition, Deconstruction, and the Hermeneutic Project*. Bloomington and Indianapolis: Indiana University Press, 1987.

Chailly, Jacques. *The Magic Flute, Masonic Opera*. Translated by Herbert Weinstock. New York: Knopf, 1971.

Chambers, Judith. *Thomas Pynchon*. Boston: Twayne Publishers, 1992.

Claggett, Marshall. *Greek Science in Antiquity*. London: Abelard-Schumann, 1957.

Collingwood, R. G. *The Idea of Nature*. Chicago: University of Chicago Press, 1949.

Colodny, Robert. *Problems and Paradoxes: The Challenge of the Quantum Domain*. Pittsburgh: University of Pittsburgh Press, 1972.

Croll, Morris W. "The Baroque Style in Prose." In *Essays in Stylistic Analysis*, edited by Howard H. Babb, 97–116. New York: Harcourt, Brace, and Company, 1972.

Crombie, A. C. *Medieval and Early Modern Science*. Garden City, N.Y.: Doubleday and Company, 1954.

Culler, Jonathan. *The Pursuit of Signs: Semiotics, Literature, Deconstruction*. Ithaca, N.Y.: Cornell University Press, 1981.

Cunnar, Eugene. "Donne's 'Valediction: Forbidding Mourning' and the Golden Compass of Alchemical Creation." In *Literature and the Occult*, edited by Luanne Frank. Arlington: University of Texas Press, 1977.

d'Abro, A. *The Rise of the New Physics*. 2 vols. New York: Dover Publications, 1951.

Danto, Arthur C. "Some Remarks on *The Genealogy of Morals.*" In *Reading Nietzsche*, edited by Robert L. Solomon and Kathleen Higgins, 13–28. New York: Oxford University Press, 1988.

Davidson, Donald. *Inquiries into Truth and Interpretation.* New York: Oxford University Press, 1984.

de Man, Paul. *Allegories of Reading: Figural Language in Rousseau, Nietzsche, Rilke, and Proust.* New Haven: Yale University Press, 1979.

——. *Blindness and Insight.* New York: Oxford University Press, 1971.

——. "Structure, Sign, and Play in the Discourse of the Human Sciences." In *The Language of Criticism and the Sciences of Man: The Structuralist Controversy*, edited by Richard Macksey and Eugenio Donato, 37–64. Baltimore: Johns Hopkins University Press, 1970.

Derrida, Jacques. *Of Grammatology.* Translated by Gayatri Spivak. Baltimore: Johns Hopkins University Press, 1976.

——. *Spurs: Nietzsche's Styles.* Translated by Barbara Harlow. Chicago: University of Chicago Press, 1979.

——. *Writing and Difference.* Translated by Alan Bass. Chicago: University of Chicago Press, 1978.

Desmonde, William. *Magic, Myth, and Money: The Origin of Money in Religious Ritual.* Glencoe, N.Y.: Free Press, 1962.

Dewey, Joseph. *In a Dark Time: The Apocalyptic Temper in the American Novel of the Nuclear Age.* West Lafayette, Indiana: Purdue University Press, 1990.

Duran, Jane. "Reliabilism, Foundationalism, and Naturalized Epistemic Justification Theory." *Metaphilosophy* 19 (April 1988):113–27.

Early, James. *Romanticism and American Architecture.* New York: A. S. Barnes and Company, 1965.

Eckley, Grace. "Exorcising the Demon Forgery, or the Forging of Pure Gold in Gaddis's *The Recognitions.*" In *Literature and the Occult*, edited by Luanne Frank. Arlington: University of Texas Press, 1977.

Eco, Umberto. *The Open Work.* Translated by Anna Canogni. Cambridge: Harvard University Press, 1989.

——. *Travels in Hyper Reality: Essays.* Translated by William Weaver. San Diego: Harcourt Brace Jovanovich, 1986.

Edwards, Harold M. "Fermat's Last Theorem." *Scientific American* 239 (October 1978): 104–22.

Einstein, Alfred. *Mozart: His Character, His Work*. London: Oxford University Press, 1961.

Eisenstein, Louis. *The Ideology of Taxation*. New York: Ronald Press, 1961.

Eliot, T. S. "Ulysses, Order, and Myth." In *Criticism: The Foundations of Modern Literary Judgement*, edited by Mark Schorer, 269–71. New York: Harcourt, Brace, and World, 1958.

Fabricius, Johannes. *The Medieval Alchemists and Their Royal Art*. Copenhagen: Rosenkilde and Bagger, 1976.

Fish, Stanley. "Interpreting the Variorum." *Critical Inquiry* 2 (1976): 470–79.

———. *Surprised by Sin: The Reader in Paradise Lost*. 2d ed. Berkeley: University of California Press, 1971.

Flake, Carol. *Redemptorama: Cultural Politics and the New Enlightenment*. New York: Anchor Press, 1984.

Fletcher, Joseph. *Situation Ethics: The New Morality*. Philadelphia: Westminster Press, 1966.

Foucault, Michel. *The Order of Things: An Archeology of the Human Sciences*. New York: Pantheon Books, 1971.

Frazer, Sir James, trans. *Apollodorus, The Library*. Cambridge: Harvard University Press, 1956.

Fries, C. C. *The Structure of English: An Introduction to the Structure of English Sentences*. New York: Harcourt, Brace, and World, 1952.

Frisby, David. *Fragments of Modernity*. Cambridge: MIT Press, 1986.

Fullerton, Kemper. "Calvinism and Capitalism." *Harvard Theological Review* 21 (1928): 163–91.

Funk, Robert Walter. *Jesus as Precursor*. Philadelphia: Fortress Press, 1975.

Gadamer, Hans-Georg. *Philosophical Hermeneutics*. Translated by David E. Linge. Berkeley: University of California Press, 1976.

———. *Truth and Method*. New York: Seabury Press, 1975.

Gaddis, William. *Carpenter's Gothic*. New York: Viking, 1985; paperback edition with corrections, New York: Penguin, 1986.

———. *J R*. New York: Knopf, 1975; paperback edition with corrections, New York: Penguin, 1993.

———. *The Recognitions*. New York: Harcourt, Brace & Co., 1955; paperback edition with corrections, New York: Penguin, 1992.

———. "The Rush for Second Place," *Harper's* 262 (April 1981): 31–39.

———. "Szyrk v. Village of Tatamount et al." *New Yorker* 63 (October 12, 1987): 44–50.

———. "Trickle-Up Economics: J R Goes to Washington." *New York Times Book Review* (October 25, 1987): 29.

Gödel, Kurt. *On Formally Undecidable Propositions*. New York: Basic Books, 1962.

Goody, Jack, and Ian Watt. "The Consequences of Literacy." In *Literacy in Traditional Societies*, edited by Jack Goody, 27–68. Cambridge: Cambridge University Press, 1966.

Graves, Robert. *The White Goddess: A Historical Grammar of Poetical Myth*. New York: Octagon Books, 1966.

Gray, Ronald. *Goethe the Alchemist: A Study of Alchemical Symbolism in Goethe's Literary and Scientific Works*. Cambridge: Cambridge University Press, 1952.

Group Mu, ed. *Collages*. Paris: Union Generale, 1978.

Grove, Lloyd. "Harnessing the Power of Babble: The Rich, Comic, Talkative Novels of William Gaddis." *Washington Post* (August 23, 1985): B1, B10.

Halio, Jay. "American Dreams." *Southern Review* 13 (1977): 837–43.

Harnack, Adolph von. *Outlines of the History of Dogma*. Translated by Edwin K. Mitchell. Boston: Beacon Press, 1957.

Hartman, Geoffrey. *The Unmediated Vision: An Interpretation of Wordsworth, Hopkins, Rilke, and Valery*. New Haven: Yale University Press, 1954.

Hassan, Ihab. *The Post-Modern Turn: Essays in Post-Modern Theory and Culture*. Columbus: Ohio State University Press, 1987.

Hayles, N. Katherine. *Chaos Bound: Orderly Disorder in Contemporary Literature and Science*. Ithaca: Cornell University Press, 1990.

———. *The Cosmic Web: Scientific Field Models and Literary Strategies in the Twentieth Century*. Ithaca: Cornell University Press, 1984.

Heidegger, Martin. *Identity and Difference*. New York: Harper and Row, 1969.

Heisenberg, Werner. *Across the Frontiers*. New York: Harper and Row, 1974.

———. *Physics and Philosophy: The Revolution in Modern Science*. New York: Harper and Row, 1958.

Holton, Gerald. "Presupposition in the Construction of Theories." *Graduate Journal* 5 (1965): 87–110.

———. *Thematic Origins of Scientific Thought*. Cambridge: Harvard University Press, 1974.

Hopkins, Gerard Manley. *Poems of Gerard Manley Hopkins*. 3d ed. Edited by W. H. Gardner. London: Oxford University Press, 1948.

Hoy, David Couzens. *The Critical Circle: Literature, History and Philosophical Hermeneutics*. Berkeley: University of California Press, 1978.

Iser, Wolfgang. *The Implied Reader: Patterns of Communication in Prose Fiction from Bunyan to Beckett*. Baltimore: Johns Hopkins University Press, 1974.

Jameson, Frederic. *Postmodernism, or, the Culture Logic of Late Capitalism*. Durham: Duke University Press, 1992.

Jastrow, Joseph, ed. *The Story of Human Error*. New York: Appleton-Century, 1936.

Jauch, J. M. *Are Quanta Real?* Bloomington: Indiana University Press, 1973.

Jaynes, E. T. "Gibbs versus Boltzmann Entropies." *American Journal of Physics* 33 (1965): 398.

Jeffers, Robinson. *The Double Axe and Other Poems*. New York: Random House, 1948.

———. *Hungerfield and Other Poems*. New York: Random House, 1954.

———. "Shine, Perishing Republic." In *The Selected Poetry of Robinson Jeffers*. New York: Random House, 1938.

Jencks, Charles. *What is Postmodernism?* New York: St. Martin's Press, 1986.

Jennings, Michael W. *Dialectical Images: Walter Benjamin's Theory of Literary Criticism*. Ithaca: Cornell University Press, 1987.

Jonas, Hans. *The Gnostic Religion: The Message of the Alien God and the Beginnings of Christianity*. 2d ed. Boston: Beacon Press, 1963.

Johnston, John. *Carnival of Repetition: Gaddis's "The Recognitions" and Postmodern Theory*. Philadelphia: University of Pennsylvania Press, 1990.

Jordan, Pascual. *Physics of the Twentieth Century*. New York: Philosophical Library, 1944.

Jung, Carl Gustav. *Psychology and Alchemy*. 2d ed. Translated by R. F. C. Hall. Princeton: Princeton University Press, 1968.

———. *Collected Works*. Edited by Herbert Read, Michael Fordham, and Gerhard Adler. Vol. 18, *The Symbolic Life*. New York: Pantheon Books, 1953.

Kermode, Frank. *The Genesis of Secrecy: On Interpretation of Narrative*. Cambridge: Harvard University Press, 1979.

Klinkowitz, Jerome. *Literary Disruptions: The Making of a Post-Contemporary American Fiction*. Urbana: University of Illinois Press, 1975.

Kuehl, John. *Alternate Worlds: A Study of Postmodern Antirealistic American Fiction*. New York: New York University Press, 1989.

Keuhl, John, and Steven Moore, eds. *In Recognition of William Gaddis*. Syracuse, N.Y.: Syracuse University Press, 1984.

Koenig, Peter (*aka* David). "Recognizing Gaddis's *Recognitions*." *Contemporary Literature* 16 (Winter 1975): 61–72.

Koyre, Alexandre. *From the Closed World to the Open Universe*. New York: Harper Torchbooks, 1958.

Kristeva, Julia. *Essays in Semiotics*. The Hague: Mouton, 1971.

Kubat, Libor, and Jiri Zeman, eds. *Entropy and Information in Science and Philosophy*. New York: Elsevier Scientific Publishing Co., 1975.

Kuhn, Thomas. *The Structure of Scientific Revolutions*. 2d ed. Chicago: University of Chicago Press, 1970.

LaCapra, Dominick. "Singed Phoenix and the Gift of Tongues: William Gaddis's *The Recognitions*." *Diacritics* 16 (Winter 1986): 33–47.

LeClair, Thomas. *The Art of Excess: Mastery in Contemporary American Fiction*. Urbana: University of Illinois Press, 1989.

———. "William Gaddis, *J R* and the Art of Excess." *Modern Fiction Studies* 27 (Winter 1981–82): 587–600.

Leverence, John. "Gaddis Anagnoresis." In *In Recognition of William Gaddis*, edited by John Kuehl and Steven Moore, 32–45. Lincoln: University of Nebraska Press, 1982.

Lovin, Robin W., and Frank Reynolds. *Cosmogony and Ethical Order: New Studies in Comparative Ethics*. Chicago: University of Chicago Press, 1985.

Lyotard, Jean-François. *The Postmodern Condition: A Report on Knowledge*. Translated by Geoff Bennington and Brian Massumi. Minneapolis: University of Minnesota Press, 1988.

McCaffery, Larry, ed. *Postmodern Fiction: A Bio-Bibliographical Guide*. Westport, Conn: Greenwood Press, 1986.

MacIntyre, Alasdair. *After Virtue*. 2d ed. Notre Dame, Ind.: University of Notre Dame Press, 1984.

McHale, Brian. *Postmodernist Fiction*. New York: Methuen, 1987.

McHoul, Alec. "Labyrinths: Writing Radical Hermeneutics and the Post-Ethical." *Philosophy Today* 31 (1987): 211–22.

McHoul, Alec, and David Wills. *Writing Pynchon: Strategies and Fictional Analysis*. Urbana: University of Illinois Press, 1900.

Maass, John. *The Gingerbread Age: A View of Victorian America*. New York: Brahnall House, 1957.

Malmgren, Carl. *Fictional Space in the Modernist and Post-Modernist American Novel*. London: Associated University Press, 1985.

Maltby, Paul. *Dissident Postmodernists: Barthelme, Coover, Pynchon*. Philadelphia: University of Pennsylvania Press, 1991.

Mandel, Ernest. *Late Capitalism*. London: New Left Books, 1975.

Manuel, Frank. *The New World of Henri Saint-Simon*. Cambridge: Harvard University Press, 1956.

———. *Portrait of Sir Isaac Newton*. Cambridge: Harvard University Press, 1972.

Matson, Floyd. *The Broken Image: Man, Science, and Society*. New York: Anchor Books, 1966.

Mellard, James. *The Exploded Form: The Modernist Novel in America*. Urbana: University of Illinois Press, 1980.

Merleau-Ponty, Jacques, ed. *The Re-Birth of Cosmology*. Translated by Helen Weaver. New York: Knopf, 1976.

Miller, Arthur L. *Imagery in Scientific Thought: Creating Twentieth-Century Physics*. Cambridge: MIT Press, 1986.

Minson, Jeffrey. *Genealogies of Morals: Nietzsche, Foucault, Donzelot, and the Eccentricity of Ethics*. New York: St. Martin's Press, 1985.

Miller, J. Hillis. *The Linguistic Moment: From Wordsworth to Stevens*. Princeton: Princeton University Press, 1985.

Milroy, James. *The Language of Gerard Manley Hopkins*. London: Andre Deutsch, 1977.

Misner, Charles W., et al. *Gravitation*. San Francisco: W. H. Freeman, 1973.

Moles, Abraham. *Information Theory and Esthetic Perception*. Translated by Joel E. Cohen. Urbana: University of Illinois Press, 1966.

Moore, Steven. *A Reader's Guide to William Gaddis's "The Recognitions."* Lincoln: University of Nebraska Press, 1982.

———. *William Gaddis.* Boston: Twayne Publishers, 1989.

———. "Chronological Difficulties in the Novels of William Gaddis." *Critique: Studies in Modern Fiction* 22 (1980): 79–81.

Motto, Marylou. *'Mined with a Motion': The Poetry of Gerard Manley Hopkins.* New Brunswick, N.J.: Rutgers University Press, 1984.

Munitz, Milton, ed. *Theories of the Universe: From Babylonian Myth to Modern Science.* Glencoe, Ill.: Free Press, 1957.

Murdoch, Iris. "The Sublime and the Good." *The Chicago Review* 13 (Autumn 1959): 42–55.

Nadeau, Robert. *Readings from the New Book on Nature: Physics and Metaphysics in the Modern Novel.* Amherst: University of Massachusetts Press, 1981.

Nagel, Ernst, and James R. Newman. *Gödel's Proof.* New York: New York University Press, 1958.

Naipaul, V. S. *The Mimic Men.* New York: Macmillan, 1967.

Needleman, Joseph. *A Sense of the Cosmos: The Encounter of Modern Science and Ancient Truth.* New York: Dalton and Company, 1977.

Newman, Ernest. *Wagner as Man and Artist.* 2d ed. New York: Knopf, 1924.

Niebuhr, Reinhold. *An Interpretation of Christian Ethics.* New York: Seabury Press, 1979.

Nietzsche, Friedrich. *The Antichrist.* In *The Portable Nietzsche,* edited by Walter Kaufmann. New York: Viking, 1968.

———. *The Birth of Tragedy from the Spirit of Music.* Translated by F. Golfing. New York: Doubleday Anchor, 1965.

———. *Ecce Homo: How One Becomes What One Is.* Translated by Walter Kaufmann (together with *On the Genealogy of Morals*). New York: Random House, 1967.

Norris, Christopher. "Image and Parable: Readings of Walter Benjamin." *Philosophy and Literature* 7 (April 1983): 15–31.

Nygren, Anders. *Agape and Eros.* Philadelphia: Western Press, 1953.

O'Brien, Denis. *Empedocles' Cosmic Cycle: A Reconstruction from the Fragments and Secondary Sources.* London: Cambridge University Press, 1969.

O'Hara, J. D. "Boardwalk and Park Place versus Chance and Peace of Mind." *Virginia Quarterly Review* 52 (Summer 1976): 523–26.

Ong, Walter. *Ramus: Method, and the Decay of Dialogue; from the Art of Discourse to the Art of Reason.* Cambridge: Harvard University Press, 1958.

Oppenheimer, Robert. *Science and the Common Understanding.* New York: Simon and Schuster, 1956.

Outka, Gene. *Agape: An Ethical Analysis.* New Haven, Conn.: Yale University Press, 1971.

Park, David. *The How and the Why: An Essay on the Origins and Development of Physical Theory.* Princeton: Princeton University Press, 1988.

Parrington, Vernon L. *Main Currents in American Thought.* New York: Harcourt, Brace, and World, 1954.

Patterson, David. *Literature and Spirit: Essays on Bakhtin and His Contemporaries.* Lexington: University Press of Kentucky, 1988.

Peters, H. F. *R. M. Rilke: The Masks and the Man.* Seattle: University of Washington Press, 1960.

Peters, W. A. M. *Gerard Manley Hopkins: A Critical Essay Toward the Understanding of his Poetry.* Chicago: Loyola University Press, 1984.

Peterson, Aage. "The Philosophy of Niels Bohr." *Bulletin of the Atomic Scientists* 19 (1963): 15–23.

Planck, Max. *The Philosophy of Physics.* New York: Norton, 1956.

Prier, Raymond Adolph. *Archaic Logic: Symbol and Structure in Heraclitus, Parmenides, and Empedocles.* The Hague: Mouton, 1976.

Purtscher, Nora. *Rilke, Man and Poet: A Biographical Study.* Westport, Conn.: Greenwood Press, 1972.

Pynchon, Thomas. *Gravity's Rainbow.* New York: Viking, 1973.

———. *V., a Novel.* Philadelphia: Lippincott, 1963.

Randall, John Hermann, Jr. *The Making of the Modern Mind.* New York: Houghton Mifflin, 1940.

Rather, L. J. *The Dream of Self-Destruction: Wagner's Ring and the Modern World.* Baton Rouge, La.: LSU Press, 1979.

Rawls, John. *A Theory of Justice.* Cambridge: Harvard University Press, 1971.

Rilke, Rainer Maria. *Duino Elegies.* Translated by Stephen Garmey and Jay Wilson. New York: Harper and Row, 1972.

———. *Duino Elegies.* Translated by J. B. Leishman and Stephen Spender. New York: Norton, 1939.

———. *Duino Elegies.* Translated by David Young. New York: W. W. Norton, 1978.

———. *Sonnets to Orpheus.* Translated by M. D. Herder. New York: W. W. Norton, 1942.

Roberts, Julien. *Walter Benjamin.* London: Macmillan Press, 1982.

Rolleston, James L. "The Politics of Quotation: Walter Benjamin's Arcades Project." *PMLA* 104 (1989): 13–25.

Rorty, Richard. *Consequences of Pragmatism.* Minneapolis: University of Minnesota Press, 1982.

———. *Philosophy and the Mirror of Nature.* Princeton: Princeton University Press, 1979.

Ross, W. D. *The Right and the Good.* Chicago: University of Chicago Press, 1930.

Rosenhein, Laurence. "Letter to Richard Pearce in Response to 'Pynchon's Endings.' " *Pynchon Notes* 17 (Fall 1985): 35–50.

Salemi, Joseph. "To Soar in Atonement: Art as Expiation in Gaddis's *The Recognitions.*" *Novel* 10, no. 2 (Winter 1977): 127–36.

Samuels, Ernest. *Henry Adams: The Major Phase.* Cambridge: Harvard University Press, 1964.

Sartre, Jean-Paul. *Existentialism.* Translated by B. Frechtman. New York: Philosophical Library Inc., 1947.

Schlant, Ernestine. *Hermann Broch.* Boston: Twayne Publishers, 1978.

———. "Hermann Broch and Modern Physics." *The Germanic Review* 53 (Spring 1978): 69–75.

Scholes, Robert. *The Fabulators.* New York: Knopf, 1976.

Shell, Marc. *The Economy of Literature.* Baltimore: Johns Hopkins University Press, 1978.

Siegle, Robert. *The Politics of Reflexivity: Narrative and the Constitutive Poetics of Culture.* Baltimore: Johns Hopkins University Press, 1986.

Smith, Harmon. "When Love Becomes Excarnate." In *Storm Over Ethics,* edited by John Bennett, James Gustafson, E. Clinton Gardner, et al. Philadelphia: United Church Press, 1967.

Spengler, Oswald. *The Decline of the West.* Translated by Charles Francis Atkinson. New York: Knopf, 1962.

Stapp, Henry. "The Copenhagen Interpretation." *American Journal of Physics* 40 (1972): 1112–21.

Stark, John. "William Gaddis: Just Recognition." *Hollins Critic* 14 (1977): 1–12.

Steiner, George. "Books: Crossed Lines." *The New Yorker* (January 26, 1976): 106–9.

Stout, Jeffrey. *Ethics After Babel: The Language of Morals and Their Discontents.* Boston: Beacon Press, 1988.

Strehle, Susan. *Fiction in the Quantum Universe.* Chapel Hill: University of North Carolina Press, 1992.

Sullivan, J. W. N. *The Limitations of Science.* New York: Viking Press, 1953.

Tawney, J. W. *Religion and the Rise of Capitalism: A Historical Study.* London: J. Murray, 1948.

Theilemans, Johan. "Gaddis and the Novel of Entropy." TREMA [Traveaux et Recherches sur le Monde Anglophone] 2 (1977): 97–107.

———. "Intricacies of Plot: Some Preliminary Remarks to William Gaddis's *Carpenter's Gothic.*" In *Studies in Honor of René Derolez,* edited by A. M. Simon-Vandenbergen, 612–21. Ghent: Seminarie voor Engelese en Oud-Germaanse Taalkunde R.U.G., 1987.

Thoreau, Henry David. *The Writings of Henry David Thoreau.* Vol. 2, *Walden.* Boston and New York: Houghton, Mifflin & Co., 1906.

Toulmin, Stephen. *The Return to Cosmology: Postmodern Science and the Theology of Nature.* Berkeley: University of California Press, 1982.

Turkle, Sherry. *Psychoanalytic Politics.* New York: Basic Books, 1978.

Weber, Max. *The Protestant Ethic and the Spirit of Capitalism.* Translated by Talcott Parsons. New York: Scribner's, 1958.

Weinberg, Steven. *Dreams of a Final Theory.* New York: Pantheon Books, 1992.

Weisenberger, Steven. "Contra Naturam?: Usury in William Gaddis's *J R.*" *Genre* 13 (Spring 1980): 93–109.

Weiss, T., ed. *Selections from the Notebooks of G. M. Hopkins.* New York: New Direction Books, 1948.

Weschler, Judith, ed. *On Aesthetics in Science.* Cambridge: MIT Press, 1978.

Westbrook, Wayne. *Wall Street in the American Novel.* New York: New York University Press, 1980.

Weyl, Herman. *The Open World*. New Haven: Yale University Press, 1932.

Wheeler, Lynde. *Josiah Willard Gibbs*. Hamdin, Conn.: Archon Books, 1970.

White, Hayden. *Metahistory: The Historical Imagination in Nineteenth-Century Europe*. Baltimore: Johns Hopkins University Press, 1973.

————. *Tropics of Discourse*. Baltimore: Johns Hopkins University Press, 1975.

White, Landeg. *V. S. Naipaul: A Critical Introduction*. London: Macmillan Press, 1975.

Whitehead, Alfred North. *Science and the Modern World*. New York: Macmillan Press, 1975.

Wiener, Norbert. *The Human Use of Human Beings: Cybernetics and Society*. Boston: Houghton Mifflin, 1954.

Wilde, Alan. *Horizons of Assent: Modernism, Postmodernism, and the Ironic Imagination*. Baltimore: Johns Hopkins University Press, 1981.

————. *Middle Grounds: Studies in Contemporary American Fiction*. Philadelphia: University of Pennsylvania Press, 1987.

Zavarzadeh, Mas'ud. *The Mythopoeic Reality: The Post-Modern American Non-fiction Novel*. Urbana: University of Illinois Press, 1976.

Ziolkowski, Theodore. "Hermann Broch and Relativity in Fiction." *Wisconsin Studies in Contemporary Literature* 8 (1967): 365–77.

Index

Absolutes, life without, 3–5, 13, 15, 17, 33, 36, 49, 74, 75, 123, 127, 132
Absurd: Camus on the, 2, 3; world as, 30
Acker, 6
Action, paramountcy of, 118, 119, 148
Adams, Henry, 18, 108
Adano de Brescia, 60
Adorno, Theodor, 43, 102
Aesthetics, politicization of, 90, 105, 106, 160n.28
Africa, "McCandless" in, 132. *See also* Kenya
After Virtue (MacIntyre), 20
Agape (n.), *agapē* and, 8, 37
Agapē, 5, 8, 17, 32, 36, 45; agape, 13, 32, 87, 99; and agape, 8, 37; alterity and, 31; *Carpenter's Gothic* vs., 123; defined, 111–12; as discipline, not feeling, 34; freemasonry and, 111; as Gaddis theme, 123; in *J R*, 35, 111–14, 122; as last best hope, 149; love as, 119 (*see also* Love, agapistic); Mozart and, 111, 112; nature of, 30; Schopenhauerian, 112. *See also* Alterity; Ethics, agapistic; Love, agapistic

"A1" (*J R*), 121
"Alberich" (*Der Ring des Nibelungen*), 93
Alchemy, 51–53, 60; art and, 53, 60; exoteric vs. esoteric, 52; Gaddis on, 157–58n.17; as Gaddis influence, 151n.9; as *Recognitions* subject, 49–51, 53–57, 59–63, 66, 67, 69, 157n.6; and science contrasted, 55
Alienation: class-related, 86; existentialism and, 30; as writer's curse, 65
Allusion(s): in *Carpenter's Gothic*, 140 (*see also* Jeffers, Robinson); Gaddis's use of, 44; in *J R*, 89, 91, 93, 105, 114 (see also *Sleepwalkers, The, J R* focus on); in *The Recognitions*, 50, 55, 67, 74–76, 82 (see also Rilke, Rainer Maria, as *Recognitions* influence)
Alterity, 31, 37, 49; *agapē* ethics and, 30; agapistic, 34, 36, 44; defined, 28; in *J R*, 88; in *The Recognitions*, 66, 73–74, 88
"Amy" (*J R*), 102, 105, 110, 111
Anacrisis, 116
Anomaly: Newtonian theory and, 22–23; as reality component, 23

"Anselm" (*The Recognitions*), 32, 33, 59
Anselm, Saint, 59
Apollo, 67
Archeus, 52–53, 66, 67
Architecture, transformational properties of, 128
Aristotle, 65
Arius, 64, 65
Arkansas, creationism rampant in, 135–36, 138–39
Art: alchemy and, 53, 60; "auratic" nature of, 89; Benjamin on, 89, 159n.10; Broch on, 105; democracy, technology, and, 99–100; finance vs., 87, 88, 94; Gaddis on, 59–60; "Gibbs" on, 97; Hollywood vs., 105; "J R" on, 119; *J R* focus on, 97, 99, 100, 105, 106, 110, 119
Arthur, Rose, 68
"Asche, Stephen." *See* "Gwyon, Wyatt"
Atonement: as *Recognitions* subtheme, 58; ritual as, 67; Saint Anselm and, 59
Augustine, Saint, 22, 31, 32, 34, 80, 86

Bach, Johann Sebastian, 119
Bakhtin, Mikhail, 5, 116, 152nn.11, 12
Barrow, John, 23
Barthes, Roland, 38, 43
"Bast, Edward" (*J R*), 33, 87, 94, 96, 97, 111–13, 118, 124; aunts of, 91, 92
Baudrillard, Jean, 86, 94
Beckett, Samuel, 44
Beethoven, Ludwig van, 112, 120
Bellah, Robert N., 1

Benjamin, Walter, 9–10, 42–45, 101–5, 123, 157n.65, 160n.28; as Gaddis influence, 43–45, 49, 157n.65; and *J R*, 89–90, 100, 102–5, 107, 110, 112, 114, 159n.10; on writers, 42–43
Benstock, Bernard, 157n.65
Bersani, Leo, 2
Bible: *Carpenter's Gothic* debt to, 129; fundamentalism "vs.," 136. *See also* Christ; Creationism; Ephesians; Genesis; Revelation
"Billy" (*Carpenter's Gothic*), 125, 129, 131, 146
Bohr, Niels, 26, 31, 39, 40, 44, 147, 154n.18. *See also* Complementarity, principle of
Booth, Katherine, 161–62n.10
"Booth, Liz" (*Carpenter's Gothic*), 125–27, 129–32, 137, 143, 149
"Booth, Paul" (*Carpenter's Gothic*), 125–27, 129–32, 162n.10
Booth, William, 161–62n.10
"Brescia, Count de" (*The Recognitions*), 60
Broch, Hermann, 13–14, 97, 105–6, 153n.29
Brontë, Charlotte, 129
"Brown, Recktall" (*The Recognitions*), 60, 62, 85, 93

Calling (divine summons), 8
Camus, Albert, 2, 3
Capitalism, 8; Benjamin on, 89, 100; as *J R* villain, 85–87, 91–97, 105, 107, 110; Marxism vs., 86; Shaw on, 93. *See also* Money
Caputo, John, 14, 31
Carnival of Repetition (Johnston), 5

Carpenter gothic, 128, 133, 161n.4
Carpenter's Gothic (Gaddis), 4, 35, 45, 123–46, 151n.3; criticism of, 152n.9; God business as element of, 156n.39; message of, 128; plot of, 124–27, 130, 132, 149; as reader's challenge, 125–26, 131–32, 145, 146; strengths of, 147; style of, 125, 127, 130, 134; thrust of, 133–34, 142. *See also* "Billy"; "Booth, Liz"; "Booth, Paul"; "Edie"; "Lester"; "McCandless"; "Ude, Elton"
"Cates, Gov." (*J R*), 116, 117
Censorship: "McCandless" vs., 135; in Texas, 136, 138–39
Chambers, Judith, 7
Chance, Gaddis on, 3, 4
Change, as natural-law element, 31
Chemistry: alchemy and, 54; thermodynamics and, 108
Child labor, as "Gibbs"/Benjamin theme, 105
Christ, 55, 68, 80; Council of Nicea on, 58; as kitsch, 35; Nietzsche on, 35, 129; pious betrayal of, 129
Christianity: Gaddis and, 5; Gnosticism vs., 68, 69; Graves on, 67; Nietzsche on, 35, 129–30; as *Recognitions* topic, 49–50, 53–59, 63, 67. *See also* Atonement; Bible; Christ; Consubstantiality; Fundamentalism, religious; Protestant ethic; Revelation
CIA (Central Intelligence Agency), as *Carpenter's Gothic* heavy, 127, 132, 133
Clement, Saint, 58

Clementine Recognitions, 68, 82
Cobalt, beer enhanced by, 94
Collaborator, reader as writer's, 36, 42–45, 73, 74, 82, 99, 110, 114, 117–18, 123, 144
Collage, Benjamesque, 42, 44, 89
Communication theory, 96
Comnes, Gregory, 160n.17
Competence: Gaddis's version of, 37; literary, 156n.44
Complementarity: epistemology and, 36; principle of, 26, 31, 44, 154n.18
Complexity theory, 23
Compressibility, algorithmic, 22–23, 26, 29
Condoms, as piano flutes, 94
Consubstantiality, in *The Recognitions*, 72, 80
Convention, agapistic love vs., 34
Cosmology, Peircian, 161n.42
"Crawley" (*J R*), 96
Creationism: in Arkansas, 135–36, 138–39; "McCandless" vs., 135
Croll, Morris W., 72–73, 79
Cross-eyed girl (*The Recognitions*), 70–72
Cybernetics, 108

Damnation, Gaddis on, 31
Dante Alighieri, 60
Danto, 155n.37
Darrow, Clarence, 135
Davidson, Donald, 30
Death: freemason position on, 111; Rilke's focus on, 76–78, 79
Dehumanization, as Gaddis fiction element, 30
"Deigh, Agnes" (*The Recognitions*), 71

Deleuze, Gilles, 5
Democracy, art, technology, and, 99–100
Depression, financial: as "Gibbs"/ Benjamin theme, 102
Derrida, Jacques, 9, 27, 37, 42, 88
Descartes, René, 18
Determinism, causal, 28; inadequacies of, 27
Dewey, John, 152n.9
Dialogue, 117; in *Carpenter's Gothic*, 125; fragmented nature of, 98–99; Gaddis's use of, 115; in *J R*, 114–18, 121, 125; Socratic, 114
Dichtung, 13
Dissonance, 115
Domination, Gaddis's resistance to, 32
Double reading, 42
Doughty, C. M., 129
"Dry Salvages, The" (Eliot), 12, 34
Duino Elegies (Rilke), 74–79, 82

"East Coker" (Eliot), 12, 149
Eckhart, Johannes, 31
Eco, Umberto, 14, 88
"Edie" (*Carpenter's Gothic*), 127
Education Research Analysts, 138
Eidos, 29
"Eigen, Tom" (*J R*), 94–97, 107, 113, 118
Einstein, Albert, 28, 155n.23
Einstein, Alfred, 111
El Greco, 80
Eliot, T. S., 12, 34, 47, 50, 149
Ellipsis: Gaddis penchant for, 72, 79, 98; Rilke's use of, 79
Empedocles, as influence on Gaddis, 106–7, 113, 151n.9
Engels, Friedrich, 87

Entropy, 160n.35; informational, 96; as *J R* subject, 107–9; "negative," 109
Ephesians (bibl.), 129
Epigraphs, "Gibbs" fascination with, 102
Epistemology, 11–12; changing face of, 26; contemporary, 14, 26, 30, 31, 36, 41, 147; ethics, narrative, and, 17–45; and knowledge, 26; Newtonian, 29. *See also* Postmodernism, epistemology of
Eros, Feuerbachian, 112
"Esme" (*The Recognitions*), 58
Essays in Semiotics (Kristeva), 27
Ethic(s): *agapē* (*see* Ethics, agapistic); agapistic, 14, 30, 31, 33, 36, 37, 44, 49, 87, 137, 149; antinomian, 29–30; Broch on, 153n.29; eclectic, 19; epistemology, narrative, and, 17–45; Gaddis on, 3, 8 (*see also* Indeterminacy, ethics of); knowledge and, 21; legalistic, 29–30; literature and, 152n.12; as narrative subject, 1, 7; originary, 30; of Peirce, 161n.42; postmetaphysical, 7; postmodern, 11; Protestant (*see* Protestant ethic); Rawls on, 19–20; situation, 30. *See also* Indeterminacy, ethics of
Ethos, 30
"Eulalio, Father" (*The Recognitions*), 58
Evil, Augustine on, 22
Excrement, Gaddis's focus on, 93–94, 119
Existentialism, 30
Experience: humility and, 31; meaning and, 11, 34; understanding and, 39–40, 118

Facts, *Carpenter's Gothic* use of, 134–45
Fatalism, 18
Faust legend, 52; as *Recognitions* subtheme, 50–51
Fermat, Pierre de, 60
Fiction, facts in, 134, 139
Fiction in the Quantum Universe (Strehle), 154n.9
Finance, art vs., 87, 88, 94
Finnegans Wake (Joyce), 51
Fish, Stanley, 156n.44
Flamenco, 62
Fletcher, Joseph, 29
Four Quartets (Eliot), 12, 153n.25. *See also* "Dry Salvages, The"; "East Coker"; "Little Gidding"
Franklin, Benjamin, 86
Frazer, James G., 49
Freemasonry, 111
Freud, Sigmund, 32, 93
Fries, C. C., 98
Frolic of His Own, A (Gaddis), 148
Fullerton, Kemper, 86
Fundamentalism, religious: *Carpenter's Gothic*'s focus on, 35, 129, 132–39, 144, 161n.4 (*see also* "Ude, Elton"). *See also* Creationism; Revelation

Gabler, Mel and Norma, 138–39
Gaddis, William: as commercial writer, 85; credo of, 145–46, 148–49; criticism of, 5–6, 151–52n.9, 152nn.10, 11 (*see also* Moore, Steven); reading, 10–12, 15, 36–37, 41–45, 49, 157n.65 (see also *Carpenter's Gothic*, as reader challenge; Collaborator, reader as writer's; Double reading; *J R*, as reader challenge; *Recognitions, The*, as

reader challenge); style of, 144; triumphs of, 147–49. See also *Agapē*; *Carpenter's Gothic*; *Frolic of His Own, A*; Indeterminacy, ethics of; *J R*; *Recognitions, The*
Gelassenheit, 31
Genesis (bibl.), Arkansas behind, 138
Genius, and talent contrasted, 33, 155n.35
Gerunds, Gaddis's reliance on, 144
"Gibbs, Jack" (*J R*), 2, 7, 32, 33, 35, 86, 87, 94–97, 99, 102–10, 112–13, 116, 118–22, 124, 146
Gibbs, Josiah Willard, 108, 109, 113
Gnosticism, 68, 69
Gödel, Kurt, 24–27, 31, 44
Goethe, Johann Wolfgang von, 92
Gold, in *Carpenter's Gothic*, 132. *See also* Money
Golden Bough, The (Frazer), 47
Goody, Jack, 64, 65
Grammar, Gaddis's liberties with, 144
Graves, Robert, 67, 69
Gravity's Rainbow (Pynchon), 7
Greed: Gaddis's focus on, 146, 148; "*J R*" as epitome of, 33; as *J R* theme, 93, 112; Wagner on, 92. *See also* Protestant ethic
Guilt, "Wyatt Gwyon" and, 62–63
Gwyion, 68
"Gwyon, Camilla" (*The Recognitions*), 48, 63, 70–72, 80
"Gwyon, Esther" (*The Recognitions*), 51, 62, 66, 74
"Gwyon, Rev." (*The Recognitions*), 48, 51, 58, 63, 72
"Gwyon, Stephen." *See* "Gwyon, Wyatt"

"Gwyon, Wyatt" (*The Recognitions*), 33, 47–48, 51, 53–54, 56, 58, 66, 70, 71, 79–83, 95, 123–24, 146, 148, 155n.35, 158n.17; child of, 63, 80, 81. *See also* Redemption, as *Recognitions* theme

Hartman, Geoffrey, 78
Hayles, Katherine, 38
Heidegger, Martin, 31, 38
Heisenberg, Werner, 25, 26, 32, 33, 39, 40, 44, 147
Heresy, Pelagian, 33
Hollywood, vs. art, 105
Homer, 57
Hopkins, Arthur, 155n.38
Hopkins, Gerard Manley, 142–45, 149
Humanism: alternative to, 140, 142; failure of, 137–39, 142, 161–62n.10; reality vs., 139
Humility, experience and, 31
Husserl, Edmund, 44
"Hyde, Major" (*J R*), 105

Imagination, Paracelsus on, 52–53
In Cold Blood (Capote), 134
Indeterminacy, 45; as *Carpenter's Gothic* element, 133–34; Einstein and, 28; epistemological theory of, 6, 26–27, 36; essential, 11, 14, 15; ethics of, 4–5, 11, 14, 17, 19, 22, 29, 32–33, 41, 73, 82, 89, 90, 118, 123, 132, 154n.20 (*see also* Postmodernism, indeterminacy of; Risk-taking; Suffering); principle of, 32, 33
Information theory, 109
'Inscape' (Hopkins), 144, 162n.23
Institute for Creation Science, 138

Integration of the Personality, The (Jung), 47, 157n.6
Intertextuality, anonymous, 43
Irenaeus, Saint, 58

"James" (*J R*), 112
Jameson, Frederic, 14, 86
Jane Eyre (C. Brontë), 129
Jaynes, E. T., 108
Jeffers, Robinson, 140–42, 144
Jennings, 152n.21
Johnston, John, 5, 152n.12
Jonas, Hans, 68
Joyce, James, 51, 64, 134; Gaddis "and," 157n.65
"J R" (*J R*), 3, 33, 93, 94, 96, 107, 116, 117, 119, 155n.36; as Stockman's replacement, 148; in "Trickle Up Economic," 148
J R (Gaddis), 2, 4, 12, 35, 41, 83, 85–122, 124; allusion in, 44; Benjamin references in, 43; Broch's influence on, 14; and *Carpenter's Gothic* compared, 137; and *Carpenter's Gothic* contrasted, 124, 125, 127–28, 133, 145; criticism of, 151–52n.9; hope offered in, 127; plot of, 87; as reader's challenge, 88–90, 98, 99, 102, 105–7, 109–10, 114, 116–19, 125, 145; strengths of, 147; style of, 45, 98, 115; and *The Recognitions* compared, 88, 98, 114; and *The Recognitions* contrasted, 88–89; thrust of, 124. *See also* "Al"; "Amy"; Art, finance vs.; "Bast, Edward"; "Cates, Gov."; "Crawley"; "Eigen, Tom"; "Gibbs, Jack"; "Hyde, Major"; "James"; "J R"; "Rhoda"; "Schepperman";

"Schramm"; "Selk, Zona"; "Vogel"; "Whiteback"
Jung, Carl, 51, 81; on alchemy, 53, 57, 66, 157n.6; as Gaddis influence, 157nn.1,6; on neurosis, 63
Justice, Rawls on, 19

Kafka, Franz, 44
Kant, Immanuel, 85
Keats, John, 33
Kenya, as _Carpenter's Gothic_ location, 132
Kingdom of God (Tolstoy), 34
"Kinkead" (_Carpenter's Gothic_), 133, 137
Klinkowitz, Jerome, 7, 9
Knowledge: epistemology and, 26; ethics and, 21; intuitive, 156n.44; love and, 31; nature of acquiring, 29; and progress, 100; reality and, 28; science and, 23; tacit, 19; truth and, 28, 42–43; understanding and, 114
Koenig, Peter/David, 151n.9, 153n.25, 157n.1
"Kripsalsingh, Ralph" (_The Mimic Men_), 140
Kristeva, Julia, 27, 43

Labor unions, as "Gibbs"/Benjamin theme, 102–5
Lacan, Jacques, 115
LaCapra, Dominick, 152n.11
Lamentation, Mount, 79
Language: dialogue and, 115; Fries on, 98; Hopkins approach to, 143–44; limitations of, 38–39; quantum science and, 40–41
Law(s): Gaddis focus on, 148; quantum, 154n.16. _See also_ Natural law

Lawyers, Gaddis's focus on, 148
Le Clair, Thomas, 152nn.9, 10
Le Corbusier (pseud. Charles Édouard Jeanneret), 128
Leishman, J. B., 76
"Lester" (_Carpenter's Gothic_), 127, 132–33
Leverence, John, 72, 151n.9, 152n.10
Light, nature of, 26
Listening, as dialogue element, 117
Liszt, Franz, 91
Literature, ethics and, 152n.12. See also _Dichtung_
"Little Gidding" (Eliot), 12
Logic: laws of, 23; nature of, 24
Love: agapistic, 32–34, 36, 63, 74, 83, 146 (see also _Agapē_); Augustine on, 31; as _Carpenter's Gothic_ victim, 35, 123–24, 126, 130, 132; ethics of, 32; Freud on, 32; as Gaddis theme, 32, 36; greed vs., 33, 92; knowledge and, 31; money vs., 8; Nietzsche on Christian, 35; novelist focus on, 7; reality and, 31; Rilke on, 76; and risk-taking, 32–33; as tax write-off, 35. See also _Agapē_
Lovin, Robin, 18
"Ludy" (_The Recognitions_), 81, 124
Luther, Martin, 8
Lyotard, Jean-François, 2

"McCandless" (_Carpenter's Gothic_), 35–36, 125–33, 135–38, 145, 146, 149. _See also_ "Kinkead"
McHoul, Alec, 11, 152n.22
MacIntyre, Alasdair, 1, 20, 153n.7
Magic Flute, The (Mozart), 111, 112

Majer, Michal, 64
Malmgren, Karl, 97, 116
MAMA (Modern Allies of Modern Art), 120
Mandel, Ernest, 87, 94
Marx, Karl, 100; in *J R*, 107
Marxism, 102, 107; Benjamin's version of, 100, 107; vs. capitalism, 86; capitalist occlusion of, 87; in *Carpenter's Gothic*, 133; in *J R*, 107, 110
Mathematics, laws of, 23
Matriarchy, as *Recognitions* recommendation, 68–69
Matrix mechanics, 40
"Max" (*The Recognitions*), 74
"May, Aunt" (*The Recognitions*), 48, 60, 72
Meaning, 44; experience and, 11, 34; Gaddis and, 6, 8, 145; of *J R*, 118; nature of narrative, 12; poststructuralist approach to, 5, 6; reader-wrought, 116 (*see also* Collaborator, reader as writer's); as *Recognitions* subtheme, 75. *See also* Understanding
Mechanics: Newtonian, 22, 26; quantum (*see* Quantum mechanics)
Milton, John, 57
Mime, Derrida on, 9
Mimesis, Gaddis and, 9; postmodernism and, 7
Mimic Men, The (Naipaul), 139, 140
Minson, Jefferey, 36
Mithraism, 48, 55, 58
Modernism, 2. *See also* Postmodernism
Money: and feces, 93; in ill odor, 92; Mozart problems with, 112; paper vs. coined, 91–92; as sacred, 86, 93–94, 112, 119; soullessness of, 8; Wagner on, 92. *See also* Capitalism; Finance
Moon, worship of, 68
Moore, G. E., 18
Moore, Steven, 32, 64, 69, 151n.6, 152nn.9, 10, 153n.32, 155n.38, 157nn.1, 6, 159n.17, 162n.18
Morality: defined, 17; of Gaddis, 18; misconceived, 19; science and, 18; and slavery, 21
Mozart, Wolfgang Amadeus, 111–12, 115, 123
Murdoch, Iris, 19, 31
Museum of Modern Art, Gaddis on, 120
Music: as highest art form, 110; in *J R*, 110–12, 114, 119–21 (*see also* Mozart, Wolfgang Amadeus; Wagner, Richard, as *J R* influence)
Myths, 49

Nadeau, Robert, 38
Naipaul, V. S., 139, 140, 142, 144, 162n.11
Narrative: ethics, epistemology, and, 17–45; reader's collaboration in, 12 (*see also* Collaborator, reader as writer's); and theory contrasted, 20–21. *See also* Dialogue
Natural law, quantum physics and, 31
Nature: imprecision of, 25; as Jeffers sanctuary, 141
Neurosis: vs. agapistic love, 34; Jung on, 63
Newman, Ernest, 159n.17
Nicea, Council of, 57, 58
Niebuhr, Reinhold, 32

Nietzsche, Friedrich, 33–35, 66, 88, 155n.37; on dissonance, 115; vs. God business, 129–30; and "perfect reader," 45
Norris, Christopher, 100
Nostalgia, delusive nature of, 20
Novels, epistemological, 6, 13, 15, 21, 106, 147. See also *Carpenter's Gothic* (Gaddis); *J R* (Gaddis); *Recognitions, The* (Gaddis); *Sleepwalkers, The* (Broch)
Number theory, 24

Of Grammatology (Derrida), 27
O'Hara, J. D., 125
Oppenheimer, J. Robert, 27, 154n.21
Oppression, in Gaddis's fiction, 30
Origen, 55–56
"Otto" (*The Recognitions*), 51–52, 60
Ouroborous, 51

Parable(s), 75, 158n.31; Benjamin aphorisms as, 102
Paracelsus, 52–53
Particle(s): light as, 26; subatomic, 25
"Pastora" (*The Recognitions*), 63, 80, 81
Pater, Walter, 110, 120
Patterson, David, 152n.12
Paul, Saint, 129
Peirce, C. S., 161n.42
Peter, Saint, 68
Peters, W. A. M., 144
Physics, Bohr on, 40; Broch and new, 105; limitations of, 25–26; Newtonian (*see* Mechanics, Newtonian); quantum (*see* Quantum physics). *See also* Light; Mechanics; Quantum physics

"Pivner" (*The Recognitions*), 56
Planck's constant, 25
Poldasky, 28, 155n.23
Politics, aestheticizing of, 160n.28
Polyani, Michael, 19
Pornography, as *Carpenter's Gothic* element, 130–31
Positivism, 14; Broch's rejection of, 13
Postethical, the, 11, 152n.22
Postmodernism: epistemology of, 12, 21–22, 33, 37, 38, 40; indeterminacy of, 11; Lyotard on, 2; and values, 14
Poststructuralism, 5, 6
Power: Christianity and, 56; as existentialist villain, 30
Presburger arithmetic, 25
Principles: of agapistic love, 31; truth and first, 40; undecidability of, 11. *See also* Values
Probability, as physics concept, 108
Protestant ethic, 8, 36, 37, 50, 139; "Gibbs" enmeshed in, 7, 35, 86, 105; impregnability of, 128; as ultimate problem, 146. *See also* Capitalism; Greed
Protestant Ethic and the Spirit of Capitalism, The (Weber), 7–8, 86
Punctuation: Gaddis's liberties with, 144; in *J R*, 98; in *The Recognitions*, 72
Pynchon, Thomas, 6, 7, 38

Quantum mechanics, 23, 25; bias of, 26; vs. causality, 155n.23; Derrida's debt to, 27; and epistemology, 31; epistemology of, 29; and indeterminacy, 28, 30; uncertainty of, 118

Quantum physics: communication element of, 40; epistemology and, 11; and indeterminacy, 119; narrative recapitulation of, 38; and natural law, 31; and postmodern epistemology, 21–22, 38; and postmodern narrative, 154n.9; *The Recognitions'* stylistic debt to, 73. *See also* Quantum mechanics; Quantum theory

Quantum theory, 38–39; and anomaly, 27; limitations on, 39; nature of, 27

Rawls, John, 19–20

Reality: knowledge and, 28; love and, 31; Newtonian concept of, 27–28; science and, 22; theories of, 26; tropes and, 45

Recognitions, The (Gaddis), 4, 31–34, 41, 47–83, 123–24, 151n.3; allusion in, 44; and *Carpenter's Gothic* compared, 137; and *Carpenter's Gothic* contrasted, 124, 127–28, 133, 145; criticism of, 5, 151–52n.9; and *Four Quartets*, 153n.25; Gaddis on, 157–58n.17, 158n.30; hope offered in, 127; and *J R* compared, 88, 98, 114; and *J R* contrasted, 88–89; as mythology manual, 47; plot of, 47–48, 70–72; as reader challenge, 50, 66, 69–76, 79–83, 85, 145; strengths of, 147; thrust of, 124; title of, 82. *See also* "Anselm"; "Brescia, Count de"; "Brown, Recktall"; Cross-eyed girl; "Deigh, Agnes"; "Esme"; "Eulalio, Father"; "Gwyon, Camilla"; "Gwyon, Es-

ther"; "Gwyon, Rev."; "Gwyon, Wyatt"; "Ludy"; "Max"; "May, Aunt"; "Otto"; "Pastora"; "Pivner"; "Sinisterra"; "Stanley"; "Valentine, Basil"

Redemption: through alchemy, 50; as Gaddis theme, 8–9, 31, 155n.38; in *J R*, 86, 87, 95, 105, 113; Jung on, 57; of Protestant ethic, 37; as *Recognitions* theme, 51–53, 62, 65, 66, 71, 74–76, 158n.17; Rilke on, 76; risks of, 33; suffering as essential to, 62. *See also* Atonement; Salvation

Redemption (Tolstoy), 35, 155n.38

Relativity, theory(-ies) of, 13, 28

Religion: as business, 35, 155–56n.39; Gaddis on, 67. *See also* Bible; *Carpenter's Gothic*; Christianity; Fundamentalism, religious; *Recognitions, The*; Revelation

Repetition, Gaddis's use of stylistic, 130

Ressentiment, 34, 155n.37

Revelation, 140; "McCandless" vs., 135, 136–37

Reynolds, Frank, 18

Rheingold, Das (Wagner), 91, 111, 160n.17

"Rhoda" (*J R*), 113, 116, 121–22

Rilke, Rainer Maria, 123; credo of, 81; as *Recognitions* influence, 74–79, 80–83, 89, 114

Ring des Nibelungen, Der (Wagner), 93, 94, 111. *See also Rheingold, Das*

Risk-taking: by Gaddis reader, 37; as *J R* element, 89; as *Recognitions* element, 74, 82

Rolleston, James L., 159n.10
Rorty, Richard, 18, 26, 154n.19
Rosenhein, Laurence, 154n.21

Salemi, Joseph, 151
Salvation, as *Recognitions* theme, 33
Salvation Army, 161n.10
Sartre, Jean-Paul, 30
"Schepperman" (*J R*), 87, 107
Schiller, Johann, 35, 156n.40
"Schramm" (*J R*), 95, 113, 118
Science: and alchemy contrasted, 55; knowledge and, 23; language of, 39; morality and, 18; reality and, 22; as *Recognitions* subject, 49–50, 53–57, 63, 67. *See also* Chemistry; Physics
Scientist, shifting image of, 28–29
Self, 28; love of, 141; world and, 27, 33; "Wyatt"/"Stephen" and, 63
Self-destructiveness, 21
"Selk, Zona" (*J R*), 87
Sex, in *Carpenter's Gothic*, 130–31, 132
Shaw, G. B., 93
"Shine, Perishing Republic" (Jeffers), 141, 162n.18
"Siegfried" (*Der Ring des Nibelungen*), 94
"Siegmund" (*Der Ring des Nibelungen*), 94
Simon Magus, 68
"Sinisterra" (*The Recognitions*), 60, 71
Slavery, morality and, 21
Sleepwalkers, The (Broch), 13–14, 153n.28; as "Gibbs" fare, 97, 106; *J R* focus on, 105
Smith, Harmon, 32

Sonnets to Orpheus (Rilke), 82
Sophia (moon goddess), 68
Spengler, Oswald, 51
"Stanley" (*The Recognitions*), 32, 58–59
Steiner, George, 88
Stevens, Wallace, 134
Stockman, David, 148
Stout, Jeffrey, 36
Strehle, Susan, 154n.9
Stupidity, Gaddis on, 35
Submission, Gaddis vs., 32
Suffering: as Gaddis fiction element, 33, 37; as *J R* element, 89; Jung on, 63, 81; Nietzsche on, 34; as *Recognitions* element, 74, 82; Rilke on, 78–79; "Wyatt Gwyon" and, 62, 63
Symbols, mathematical: as words, 40
Syntax, Gaddis's liberties with, 144

"Tamino" (*The Magic Flute*), 111
Technology: art, democracy, and, 99–100
Teleology, Benjamin's rejection of, 102
Texas, book banning in, 136, 138
Theilemans, Johannes, 152n.9
Theory, logic of, 24–25
Theory of Justice, A (Rawls), 19
Theses on the Philosophy of History (Benjamin), 102
Thoreau, Henry David, 3–4, 63, 81, 95–96, 117
Tillich, Paul, 57
Titian, 80
Tolstoy, Leo, 34–35, 155n.38, 158nn.30, 31
Toulmin, Stephen, 18

Transcomputability, algorithmic, 23
Transformation: in *Carpenter's Gothic*, 126; as *Recognitions* theme, 83; as Rilke theme, 77–83
Travels in Arabia Deserta (Doughty), 129
Tropes, and reality, 45
Truth: Benjamin on, 100, 102; first principles and, 40; Gaddis on, 35; knowledge and, 28, 42–43; "Lester" on, 133; meta-ethical, 31; "revelation" vs., 135

"Ude, Elton" (Carpenter's Gothic), 125, 126, 129, 162n.10
Ulysses (Joyce), 134
Uncertainty principle, 25
Undecidability, centrality to thinking of, 27
Understanding: complementary nature of, 44; dialogic, 114; experience and, 39–40, 118; knowledge and, 114; phenomenology of, 118
Universe: death of, 108; nature of, 23; Newtonian view of, 22–23
U.S. Department of Defense, Gaddis as publicist for, 85

"Valentine, Basil" (*The Recognitions*), 48, 50, 55, 58–62, 69, 71, 80
Values: Broch on, 13; facts and, 18; money vs. traditional, 87; postmodernism and, 14
Virgil, 57

Virtue, agapistic love and, 31
"Vogel" (*J R*), 119, 120

Wagner, Richard, 92; as Gaddis influence, 151n.9; as *J R* influence, 91–94, 110, 112, 159n.17; Nietzsche's admiration of, 115. See also *Ring des Nibelungen, Der*
Walden (Thoreau), 3–4
Walden Pond, 4
War and Peace (Tolstoy), 158n.30
Wave, light as, 26
Weapons, toy, 94
Weber, Max, 7, 8, 86
Weisenberger, Steven, 151n.9
Wheeler, John, 28
"Whiteback" (*J R*), 116, 117
White Goddess, The (Graves), 47, 67
Whitehead, Alfred North, 64
Wiener, Norbert, 96, 108–9
Wilde, Alan, 11, 152n.23
Wilde, Oscar, 99, 102
"Wise Men in Their Bad Hours" (Jeffers), 140–41, 162n.15
Words, mathematical symbols as, 40
Wotan, 34, 35, 37, 93
Wright, Frank Lloyd, 128
Writing, Naipaul on, 140
"Wyatt." *See* "Gwyon, Wyatt" (*The Recognitions*)
Wyatt, Ian, 64, 65

"Yák, Mr." *See* "Sinisterra" (*The Recognitions*)

Zavarzadeh, Mas'ud, 134